ST. AUGUSTINE

THE LORD'S
SERMON ON THE MOUNT

DE SERMONE DOMINI IN MONTE

Ancient Christian Writers

THE WORKS OF THE FATHERS IN TRANSLATION

EDITED BY

JOHANNES QUASTEN, S. T. D.
Professor of Ancient Church History and Christian Archaeology

JOSEPH C. PLUMPE, Ph. D.
Associate Professor of New Testament Greek and Ecclesiastical Latin

The Catholic University of America
Washington, D. C.

No. 5

ST. AUGUSTINE

THE LORD'S
SERMON ON THE MOUNT

TRANSLATED

BY

THE VERY REVEREND
JOHN J. JEPSON, S. S., Ph. D.
Vice-Rector of Theological College
Catholic University of America
Washington, D. C.

WITH

AN INTRODUCTION AND NOTES BY THE EDITORS

NEWMAN PRESS

New York, N.Y./Ramsey, N.J.

Nihil Obstat:
  Johannes Quasten, S.T.D.
    Censor Deputatus

Imprimatur:
  Patricius A. O'Boyle, D.D.
    Archiepiscopus Washingtonensis
      die 2 Aprilis 1948

Library of Congress
Catalog Card Number: 78-62451

ISBN: 0-8091-0246-3

PUBLISHED BY PAULIST PRESS
Editorial Office: 1865 Broadway, New York, N.Y. 10023
Business Office: 545 Island Road, Ramsey, N.J. 07446

PRINTED AND BOUND IN THE UNITED STATES OF AMERICA

CONTENTS

ST. AUGUSTINE

THE LORD'S
SERMON ON THE MOUNT

INTRODUCTION

Among the sermons of the Lord found in the New Testament there is none of such importance as the Sermon on the Mount, that is, the sermon which the Lord addressed to His disciples and the crowds near Capharnaum in the mountainous region north of Lake Genesareth.[1] It is small wonder that St. Augustine should dedicate a special treatise to this sermon in order to assist those who sought an authentic interpretation of its challenging content. The intimate relationship between ethics and religion as it appears in this sermon had a special appeal for St. Augustine, and the importance of the leading idea, that God is our Father and we are His children, prevailed upon him to analyze its contents thoroughly. He who had investigated all philosophical systems of his times in the search of truth, found here a complete rule of life, the best philosophy of life. He wrote his work during the years 393 to 396 when he served as a priest at Hippo. It is possible that the care for the souls entrusted to him was one of the reasons why Augustine became especially interested in the Sermon on the Mount, containing as it does the solution of all problems of human life. Later, during the years 426 and 427, he reviewed the treatise and set down a very considerable number of criticisms and corrections in his *Retractationes* (1. 19).

The New Testament has two versions of the Sermon on the Mount which differ considerably from each other as regards length and extent.[2] St. Matthew offers the text in chapters 5-7, St. Luke in chapter 6, verses 20-49. Augustine uses the version of St. Matthew as the basis of his treatise which comprises two books.

In the first book he answers the question of the true meaning of the Sermon on the Mount. This question has remained an object of lively discussion up to our own times. It was asked: Is it humanly possible to put the Sermon on the Mount into practice? Many theological authors believed that they had found the correct answer to this question by limiting the sermon to the extent that it is meant for only a chosen few and not for the rank and file, that its demands do not represent commandments but counsels for those aiming at perfection.[8] The representatives of the eschatological school[4] find the demands of the Sermon on the Mount too radical to be meant for all times and all generations. They think that these moral obligations applied only to the early Christians, to whom, since they believed that the end of the world was impending, the worldly goods of culture and civilization meant nothing. Again, there are those[5] who are of the opinion that the moral demands in the Sermon on the Mount are purposely exaggerated to a point where they appear paradoxical and senseless, in order to make man feel that he should indeed fulfill these obligations, but that he is simply unequal to the task. The result supposed is that man will thus be led to do penance and to believe and so will be saved. According to others,[6] Jesus never intended in His Sermon on the Mount to replace the Law of the Old Testament by a new law. Therefore the ethics of the Sermon on the Mount have no literal meaning, but are only the expression of a noble way of thinking. L. N. Tolstoi[7]—to quote a name respected by millions—regards the Sermon on the Mount as the final judgment passed on all culture and civilization.

After noting all these modern attempts of interpretation it

is most interesting to study the reflection given to this sermon by the greatest exponent of moral theology in Christian antiquity. St. Augustine does not regard the ethical content of this sermon as a moral code for a select few but as a perfect rule or pattern of Christian life. He does not limit its demands to counsel or advice for a better class of Christians, but regards its precepts as a standard and mold of life for every follower of Christ. The true Christian can find in this sermon a solution for all problems which pertain to human life. St. Augustine is so far from seeing only a counsel in the moral demands of the Sermon on the Mount that he compares it with the giving of the Law on Mount Sinai. Thus the mountain which the Lord ascended is to him a symbol of the exalted position from which the Lord gave the greater legislation of the New Law as contrasted with the minor precepts of the Old Law promulgated on Mount Sinai. Augustine is firmly convinced that the Lord intended to replace the Law of the Old Testament by a new one. For this reason he emphasizes the fact that the difference between the commandments of Sinai and those of the Sermon on the Mount is not only a difference of application and permanence but also of quality. Fear was the impulse of man in the ancient dispensation, but love motivates the follower of Christ in the new. The Jewish people were not as yet mature to serve in love, therefore they served in fear. In line with this was the fact that the Law of the Old Testament was severe and treated men like slaves. Augustine mentions that the Old Law was pedantic, external, filled with ritual, ceremonial precepts. Fear of punishment caused men to act according to the Law. The impulse of love was lacking and so was serenity of conscience. Of course, the Law of this dispensation was also a law of God. But it was made for one who is a slave and not yet motivated by love. But in God's Providence mankind could not be kept in this servitude forever. And thus the time of the New Law came. Jesus, the new law-giver, appears on the mountain surrounded by His people in order to promulgate the new law of love. Far from being destructive of the good of the past, this New Law embodied the greatest progress which culture and civilization has ever made.

The Sermon on the Mount begins with the Beatitudes (Matthew 5. 3-12) which constitute so many conditions for the entrance into God's kingdom and contain the entire moral code of the New Testament. It is interesting to note that St. Augustine reduces the eight Beatitudes as enumerated by Matthew to seven. He feels justified to do so, stating that the eighth Beatitude which concludes the series returns to the starting-point and is practically identical with the first. Both, the first and the eighth, mention the kingdom of God as a reward. The seventh Beatitude reaches the highest stage of perfection,[8] signifying as it does, peace; and peace is identical with wisdom. There is nothing more perfect than wisdom because it is contemplation of truth which in turn tranquilizes the whole of man and assumes the likeness of God. St. Augustine reveals here the great passion of his whole life, the quest and love of truth. To him the climax of all piety is the contemplation of truth, that is, wisdom. The seven Beatitudes are seven stages of perfection. Hence he states at the end: " Seven in number, therefore, are the things which lead to perfection " (1. 3. 10).

It is one of St. Augustine's favorite thoughts that wisdom is the highest stage of perfection, while fear of God is the first stage or beginning of it. Augustine was too much of a Neoplatonist not to be convinced that knowledge and virtue go together, that *contemplatio* ranks higher than *actio*.[9] But to him this knowledge is *sapientia*, is the knowledge of divine things in contradistinction to *scientia*, the knowledge of human things. In his work *On the Trinity* St. Augustine investigates the difference between these two kinds of knowledge and emphasizes the superior value of wisdom: " If, therefore, this is the right distinction between wisdom and knowledge, that the intellectual cognition of eternal things pertains to wisdom, but the rational cognition of temporal things to knowledge, it is not difficult to judge which is to be esteemed more and which less. . . . No one doubts that the former is to be preferred to the latter." [10]

However, it is even more interesting that St. Augustine compares the seven Beatitudes with the seven Gifts of the Holy Ghost. To this end he reverses the order of the seven Gifts and remarks that each one of them can be compared with the corresponding number of the seven Beatitudes. Thus a gradually ascending order of seven stages of piety can be found in the Beatitudes as well as in the seven Gifts of the Holy Ghost; and St. Augustine gains the following scheme:

BEATITUDES	GIFTS OF THE HOLY GHOST
1 Humility	1 Fear of the Lord
2 Meekness	2 Godliness
3 Sorrow	3 Knowledge
4 Justice	4 Fortitude
5 Mercy	5 Counsel
6 Purity	6 Understanding
7 Peace	7 Wisdom

In a thorough analysis St. Augustine compares each corresponding set of numbers in these two columns. One could be tempted to regard this comparison as a mere play with numbers and ciphers, a sort of theological legerdemain. However, there is a very important theological doctrine at the basis of this exposition. According to patristic theology the New Law is essentially an internal law, is nothing else than the presence of the Holy Spirit in the human heart. Irenaeus [11] describes repeatedly the true Law of the new dispensation as the inhabitation of the Holy Spirit who teaches and sanctifies the Christian by love. The roots of this theological doctrine can be found in St. Paul's idea of the " Law of Faith " which the Apostle calls " the glory of the Christians " and which he opposes to the " Law of Works." In his *Epistle to the Romans* (8. 27) he calls the New Law the " Law of the Spirit of life." This idea is the point of departure for St. John Chrysostom. According to him the New Law is the Holy Spirit Himself who writes the content of the Law into the tables of the heart.[12] St. Augustine found the idea so important that he dedicated a special treatise to this topic, entitled *De Spiritu et littera*; in it the following sentences occur:

What else are the laws of God written by God Himself into our hearts than the presence itself of the Holy Ghost? By His presence love is poured into our hearts which is the fullness of the law.[13]

Thomas Aquinas [14] has incorporated this patristic doctrine in moral theology and Suarez and Driedo have treated it extensively. Augustine is so convinced of this idea that he tries to match the Beatitudes with the Gifts of the Holy Ghost by reducing the former to seven and reversing the order of the latter. He is convinced that the New Law promulgated in the Sermon on the Mount is essentially a living force which God gives to the soul in the inhabitation of the Holy Ghost and Sanctifying Grace. The seven Gifts of the Holy Ghost accompany this inhabitation and grace; and thus St. Augustine makes the Beatitudes correspond to the Gifts of the Holy Ghost and regards both of them as seven stages of grace.[15]

St. Augustine then compares the Old Law with the New and points out especially the instances in which the New Law surpasses the Old. Thus he speaks of marriage and divorce, of love of enemy and of oaths, of the concept of sin and the sin against the Holy Ghost.

While in the first book of the treatise St. Augustine interprets the fifth chapter of St. Matthew, in the second book he deals with the sixth and seventh chapters of this Gospel. He treats here especially of prayer so that the Book contains a condensed theology of prayer. In the heart of this theology we find a charming interpretation of the Lord's Prayer.[16] Here one of St. Augustine's favorite topics appears, the Fatherhood of God of which the Our Father is the simplest, truest expression in words.

Again, it is most interesting that St. Augustine here resumes the principal idea of the first book of his work by comparing the seven petitions of the Lord's Prayer with the seven Beatitudes. However, after what we have said above, this can be readily understood. Since according to St. Augustine the first seven Beatitudes are stages of grace they correspond to the seven petitions of the Our Father inasmuch as they ask for the coming of the Kingdom of God. Explaining the seven petitions, St. Augustine finds an occasion to treat the duties of man towards God and his neighbor. Here again the theme of the whole work appears that in all there is grace and that the child of God acts under the impulse of grace in joy and freedom, devoid of fear and motivated by love.

Throughout the entire work St. Augustine is anxious to make clear what is the innermost principle and the deepest root of all Christian ethics. Thus his work, *The Lord's Sermon on the Mount*, remains an important contribution to the history of ethics in general and of moral theology in particular. Scholastic theologians of the Middle Ages [17] have used St. Augustine's ideas as here set forth regarding the Beatitudes, the Gifts of the Holy Ghost and the petitions of the Lord's Prayer, to build up a complete system of Christian perfection which found its consummation in the writings of St. Bonaventure and St. Thomas Aquinas.[18]

*   *   *

The text here used is that published by the Benedictines of St. Maur in their monumental edition of St. Augustine's works at the close of the seventeenth century and reprinted by J. P. Migne, *Patrologia Latina* 34 (1845) 1229-1308. The following earlier translations may be noted:

Bassi, D., *Il discorso della montagna* (Corona Patrum Salesiana, Series latina 1, Turin 1935).[19]

Devoille, A., *Explication du Sermon de la Montagne*, in *Oeuvres complètes de Saint Augustin* 5 (sous la direction de M. Raulx, Bar-le-Duc 1867) 257-317.

Findlay, W., *Our Lord's Sermon on the Mount*, in *The Works of Aurelius Augustine, Bishop of Hippo* 8 (edited by M. Dods, Edinburgh 1873) 1-132; revised and edited by D. S. Schaff (A Select Library of the Nicene and Post-Nicene Fathers of the Christian Church, First Series 6, New York 1903) 1-63.

Neri, B., *Il sermone del monte* (Bibliotheca Agostiniana, Florence 1928).

BOOK ONE

Explanation of the First Part of the Lord's Sermon on the Mount, Contained in the Fifth Chapter of Matthew

CHAPTER 1

*The Sermon on the Mount is the perfect pattern
of the Christian life. The poor in spirit.*

If a person will devoutly and calmly consider the sermon which our Lord Jesus Christ spoke on the mount, as we read it in the Gospel according to Matthew, I think he will find in it, as measured by the highest norms of morality, the perfect pattern of the Christian life. We dare to promise this not without warrant: it is a conclusion based on the spoken words of the Lord Himself. For the conclusion of the sermon is so phrased as to make it apparent that it embraces all the directives we need for life. For thus He says: *Every one, therefore, that heareth these my words and doth them, I shall liken him to a wise man that built his house upon a rock: the rain fell, the floods came, the winds blew and they beat upon that house; and it fell not, for it was founded on a rock. And every one that heareth these my words and doth them not, I shall liken him to a foolish man that built his house upon the sand: the rain fell, the floods came, the winds blew and they beat upon that house; and it fell, and great was the fall thereof.*[1]

Since, therefore, He did not say only "that heareth my words," but said this with an addition, stating: *that heareth these my words*, He sufficiently indicated, it seems to me, that these words which He spoke on the mount, so perfectly shape the life of those who wish to live according to them as deservedly to be likened to one who built upon a rock. I remark this in order to make it clear that this sermon has been made up of all the precepts by which Christian life has vitality. In the proper place there will be a fuller comment on this section.

2. Now, then, the sermon begins with these words: *But when He had seen the many crowds, He went up into a mountain, and when He was set down, His disciples came unto Him; and opening His mouth, He taught them, saying* . . . (5. 1 f.).

If the question is raised, what is meant by the " mountain," we can well see that it stands for the greater precepts of righteousness, the lesser ones of course being those which were given to the Jews. But here it is one and the same God who through His holy Prophets and servants, by a disposition of time that was perfectly ordered, gave the lesser precepts to a people who as yet had to be controlled by fear, and through His Son the greater ones to a people for whom it was now expedient to be free in love. In the giving of the lesser to the less and of the greater to the greater, the giving is by Him who alone knows to give to the human race the remedy suitable to the times. Nor is it surprising that the greater precepts are given on account of the kingdom of heaven and the lesser were given on account of an earthly kingdom by that one same God who made heaven and earth. Therefore, concerning this righteousness which is greater, we have the statement by the Prophet: *Thy justice is as the mountains of God;* [2] and this illustrates well that one teacher only, one who alone is competent to teach doctrines so weighty, teaches on a mountain. Further, He teaches sitting down—which has reference to the dignity of the teaching office. *And His disciples come unto Him* that for the hearing of His words they might be the nearer even in body who were approaching moreover in soul to fulfill His precepts. *And opening His mouth He taught them, saying. . . .* This circumlocution which runs: *And opening His mouth,* perhaps intimates by the mere suggestion of a pause that the sermon is to be somewhat longer than usual; unless, possibly, it be not without significance that now He is said to have opened His mouth, when in the Old Law it was His wont to open the mouth of the Prophets.

3. Now, what does He say? *Blessed are the poor in spirit, for theirs is the kingdom of heaven* (3). We read in the Scriptures concerning the craving for temporal things: *All is vanity and presumption of spirit.* [3] *Presumption of spirit* means boldness and haughtiness. In common parlance, too, the haughty are said to have " high spirits "; and rightly, since spirit is also called " wind." Whence it is written: *Fire, hail, snow, ice, stormy wind.* [4] And who has not heard the haughty spoken of as " inflated," blown up, as it were, with wind? So, too, the expression of the Apostle: *Knowledge puffeth up, but charity edifieth.* [5] For this reason *the poor in spirit* are rightly understood here as the humble and those who fear God, that is, those who do not have an inflated spirit. And there could be no more felicitous beginning of blessedness, whose ultimate goal is perfect wisdom: *The fear of the Lord is the beginning of wisdom.* [6] Whereas, on the contrary, we have the attribution: *The*

beginning of all sin is pride.[7] Let, therefore, the haughty seek and love the kingdom of the earth; but *Blessed are the poor in spirit, for theirs is the kingdom of heaven.*

CHAPTER 2

The other Beatitudes.

4. *Blessed are the meek, for they shall possess the land by inheritance.*[8] The land I take in the sense of the Psalm: *Thou art my hope, my portion in the land of the living.*[9] It stands for something solid, the stability of an undying inheritance, where the soul in a state of well-being rests as in its natural environment, as the body does on earth; and thence draws its food, as the body from the earth. This is the life and rest of the Saints. The meek are those who yield before outbursts of wickedness and do not resist evil, but overcome evil with good.[10] Therefore let those who are not meek struggle and contend for earthly and temporal things; but *blessed are the meek, for they shall possess the land by inheritance* from which they cannot be expelled.

5. *Blessed are the mourners, for they shall be comforted* (5). Mourning is sadness for the loss of dear ones. But when people turn to God, they dismiss what they cherished as dear in this world; for they do not find joy in those things which before rejoiced them; and until there comes about in them the love for what is eternal, they feel the sting of sadness over a number of things. They, therefore, will be comforted by the Holy Spirit, who especially for this reason is named the Paraclete, that is, the Consoler, that disregarding the temporal they may enjoy eternal happiness.

6. *Blessed are they that hunger and thirst after justice, for they shall have their fill* (6). Here He means those who love the true and unshakable good. The food with which they will be filled is the food that the Lord Himself mentions: *My meat is to do the will of my Father,*[11] which is righteousness; and the water, of which whoso shall drink, as He Himself says, *it shall become in him a fountain of water springing up into life everlasting.*[12]

7. *Blessed are the merciful, for mercy shall be shown them* (7). He pronounces them blessed who come to the aid of the needy, since it is paid back to them so that they are freed from distress.

8. *Blessed are the clean of heart, for they shall see God* (8). How senseless, therefore, are they who look for God with bodily eyes, since He is seen by the heart, as elsewhere it is written: *And seek Him in simplicity of heart.*[13] For this is a clean heart, one that is a simple heart; and as the light of this world cannot be seen save with sound eyes, so God cannot be seen unless that is sound by which He can be seen.

9. *Blessed are the peacemakers, for they shall be called the children of God* (9). Perfection lies in peace, where nothing is at war; and the children of God are peaceful for the reason that no resistance to God is present, and surely children ought to bear a likeness to their father. And they are at peace with themselves who quell all the emotions of their soul and subject them to reason, that is, to the mind and spirit, and have their carnal passions well under control; these make up the kingdom of God. In this kingdom everything is in such perfect order that the noblest and most excellent elements in man control without opposition the other elements which are common to us and animals. Moreover,

what is most distinguished in man—mind and reason—is
subject to a higher being, which is Truth itself, the only-
begotten Son of God; for it cannot control the lower unless
it puts itself in subjection to its superior. And this is the
peace which is given on earth to men of good will; [14] this is
the life of a man who is rounded out and perfect in wisdom.
From a kingdom of this sort enjoying greatest peace and order
has been cast out the Prince of this world [15] who lords it over
the perverse and disorderly. With this peace set up and
established in the soul, whatever onslaughts he who has been
cast out makes against it from without, he but increases the
glory which is according to God. He weakens nothing in that
structure but by the very ineffectiveness of his machinations
reveals what strength has grown within. Hence it follows:
*Blessed are they that suffer persecution for justice' sake, for
theirs is the kingdom of heaven.* (10).

CHAPTER 3

*The Beatitudes mark the stages traversed towards
perfection.*

10. These, then, are His maxims—eight in all. He now
addresses the rest to those who were present, saying: *Blessed
will ye be when they shall revile you and persecute you* (11).
The earlier maxims He directed to a general audience; for He
did not say, " Blessed are the poor in spirit, for *yours* is the
kingdom of heaven "; but He said, *for theirs is the kingdom
of heaven*; not, " Blessed are the meek, for *you* shall possess
the land "; and so for the others down to the eighth, where
He said: *Blessed are they that suffer persecution for justice'*

sake, for theirs is the kingdom of heaven. Now, from this point He began a direct address to His audience; although what had gone before had reference also to those who made up His audience, just as what is to follow, though seemingly addressed to His immediate audience, has reference also to those who were not there and to those of a future time. Therefore we are to give good heed to the number of those maxims. For blessedness starts with humility: *Blessed are the poor in spirit,* that is, those who are not puffed up, whose soul is submissive to divine authority, who stand in dread of punishment after this life despite the seeming blessedness of their earthly life. The soul next makes itself acquainted with Sacred Scripture according to which it must show itself meek through piety, so that it may not make bold to censure what appears a stumbling block to the uninstructed and become intractable by obstinate argumentation. The soul now begins to realize what a hold the world has on it through the habits and sins of the flesh. In this third step, then, wherein is knowledge, there is grief for the loss of the highest good through clinging to the lowest.

In the fourth step there is hard work. The soul puts forth a tremendous effort to wrench itself from the pernicious delights which bind it. Here there must be hunger and thirst for righteousness, and there is great need for fortitude, for not without pain is the heart severed from its delights.

At the fifth step it is sugges.   to those who are continuing their energetic efforts how they may be helped to master their situation. For unless one is helped by a superior power, he is incapable of freeing himself by his own efforts from the bonds of misery which encompass him. The suggestion given is a just proposition: If one wishes to be helped by a more powerful person, let him help someone who is weaker in a field wherein he himself holds an advantage. Hence, *Blessed are the merciful, for mercy will be shown them.*

The sixth step is cleanness of heart from a good consciousness of works well done, enabling the soul to contemplate that supreme good which can be seen only by a mind that is pure and serene.

Finally, the seventh step is wisdom itself, that is, contemplation of the truth, bringing peace to the whole man and effecting a likeness to God; and of this the sum is, *Blessed are the peacemakers, for they shall be called the children of God.*

The eighth maxim returns, as it were, to the beginning, because it shows and commends what is perfect and complete. Thus, in the first and the eighth the kingdom of heaven is mentioned: *Blessed are the poor in spirit, for theirs is the kingdom of heaven*; and, *Blessed are they that suffer persecution for justice' sake, for theirs is the kingdom of heaven*—when now it is said: *Who shall separate us from the love of Christ? Shall tribulation? or distress? or persecution? or hunger? or nakedness? or danger? or the sword?* [16]

Seven in number, therefore, are the things which lead to perfection. The eighth maxim throws light upon perfection and shows what it consists of, so that, with this maxim beginning again, so to speak, from the first, the two together may serve as steps toward the perfection of the others also.

CHAPTER 4

The Beatitudes and the sevenfold Gifts of the Holy Spirit. The mystical number eight.

11. To these seven steps and maxims there corresponds, so it seems to me, the sevenfold operation of the Holy Spirit

spoken of by Isaias.[17] But the precedence is different: there the enumeration begins with the more excellent, here, with the more lowly. For in Isaias wisdom leads the list and the fear of the Lord brings it to a close; but *the fear of the Lord is the beginning of wisdom.*[18] Hence, if we count them in an ascending gradation, the first in Isaias is the fear of the Lord; the second, godliness; the third, knowledge; the fourth, fortitude; the fifth, counsel; the sixth, understanding; the seventh, wisdom.

The fear of the Lord corresponds with the humble, of whom it is said in the present text: *Blessed are the poor in spirit*—that is, those not conceited, not proud; to whom the Apostle says: *Be not highminded, but fear* [19]—that is, do not be haughty.

Godliness corresponds to the meek, for he who seeks in a godly frame of mind honors Holy Scripture and does not find fault with what as yet he does not understand, and therefore he does not oppose it—which is to be meek. Whence it is here said: *Blessed are the meek.*

Knowledge corresponds to those who mourn, who have come to learn through Scripture with what evils they are held in fetters which aforetime in their ignorance they sought as good things and useful. Of these it is here said: *Blessed are they that mourn.*

Fortitude corresponds to those who hunger and thirst, for they labor in a desire for the joy that comes from what is truly good and in an effort to stem their love for the earthly and corruptible. Hence of them it is said: *Blessed are they that hunger and thirst after justice.*

Counsel corresponds to the merciful; for this is the one means of evading burdensome evils: that we forgive as we wish to be forgiven and that we help others to the best of our ability as we hope to be helped in our need. Accordingly it is said here: *Blessed are the merciful.*

Understanding corresponds to the clean of heart—a cleansed eye, so to speak, whereby can be discerned what the bodily *eye hath not seen, nor ear heard, neither hath it entered into the heart of man;* [20] of whom it is here said: *Blessed are the clean of heart.*

Wisdom corresponds to the peacemakers in whom everything is in order and there is no emotion to rebel against reason,[21] but all things obey the spirit of man just as it obeys God; of whom it is here said: *Blessed are the peacemakers.*

12. Now, the one reward, which is the kingdom of heaven, is designated variously by a title congruous with the several steps.

In the first, as was fitting, there was set up the kingdom of heaven, which is the perfect and highest wisdom of the rational soul. Hence it was said: *Blessed are the poor in spirit, for theirs is the kingdom of heaven,* as if it were said: *The fear of the Lord is the beginning of wisdom.*

To the meek an inheritance was given as to those carrying out their Father's will in a dutiful spirit: *Blessed are the meek, for they shall possess the land as by inheritance.* To those who mourn, consolation, as to those who realize what they have lost and in what lowly condition they are: *Blessed are they that mourn, for they shall be comforted.* To the hungry and thirsty, abundance, like a repast for those who are at work and are energetically striving for their salvation: *Blessed are they that hunger and thirst after justice, for they shall have their fill.* To the merciful, mercy, as to those who act on the true and best counsel in order that what they do to the weaker may be accorded them by the stronger: *Blessed are the merciful, for they shall obtain mercy.* To the clean of heart, the faculty of seeing God, as to those possessing a clear-sighted eye to take in eternal realities: *Blessed are the clean of heart, for they shall see God.* To the peacemakers, the likeness of God, as to the perfectly wise and conformed to the image of God through the rebirth of the renewed man: *Blessed are the peacemakers, for they shall be called the children of God.* And these things can be realized even in this life, as we believe the Apostles realized them.[22] And certainly no words can express that complete transformation into the likeness of angels which is promised for the afterlife.

Blessed, therefore, are they that suffer persecution for justice' sake, for theirs is the kingdom of heaven. This eighth maxim, which harks back to the first, and announces the perfected man, is perhaps expressed in type in the Old Testament by circumcision on the eighth day and by the resurrection of the Lord after the Sabbath which is at once the eighth day of the week and the first; also by the celebration of the octave which we keep on occasion of the rebirth of the renewed man; [23] and by the very name Pentecost. For to the number seven multiplied seven times—making forty-nine—an eighth is added, as it were, so that we have fifty and in a way return to the beginning.[23a] It was on this day that the Holy Spirit was sent by whom we are brought into the kingdom of heaven and receive our inheritance and are consoled, are fed, and obtain mercy, and are cleansed, and made at peace; and, thus made perfect, we bear for truth and righteousness whatever annoyances we have to endure from without.

CHAPTER 5

Suffering for Christ.

13. *Blessed shall ye be,* He said, *when they will revile you and persecute you and speak all that is evil against you, untruly, for my sake. Be glad and rejoice, for your reward is great in heaven* (11 f.). Let him notice this—whoever seeks the delights of this world and the advantage of temporal things ostensibly as a Christian—that our blessedness is within the soul; just as it is said with prophetic speech concerning the soul of a member of the Church: *All the beauty of the king's daughter is within.*[24] For from without are promised revilings and persecutions and calumnies; though for these the reward in heaven is great, which is experienced in the heart of those who endure them, who can already say: *We glory in tribulation, knowing that tribulation worketh patience, and patience trial, and trial hope, and hope confoundeth not, because the charity of God is poured forth in our hearts by the Holy Ghost who is given to us.*[25] It is not the enduring of these things that brings reward, but bearing them for the name of Christ not only with unruffled soul but even with rejoicing. For many a heretic—under the name of Christian deceiving souls—has suffered many a like persecution; but such are excluded from the promised reward[26] for this reason, that not only was it said: *Blessed are they that suffer persecution,* but this proviso was attached: *for justice' sake.* But where there is no healthy faith there can be no justice; *for the just man liveth by faith.*[27] Nor may schismatics promise themselves any share in this reward, because in like manner where charity is not, justice cannot be;

for the love of neighbor worketh no evil.[28] If they had this charity they would not rend *the body of Christ which is the Church.*[29]

14. Here the question may be raised, what difference there is in His saying, *when they shall revile you,* and, *they shall speak all that is evil against you*—since to revile is precisely this, to speak evil. Well, in one way an evil word may be hurled with insult to the face of him who is ill-spoken against, as it was said to our Lord: *Do we not say truly that Thou art a Samaritan and hast a devil?* [30] in another way, when the good name of someone is assailed in his absence, as again it is written of Him: *Some said, " He is a prophet "; but others said, " No, but He seduceth the people." * [31] Again, to persecute is to use violence or seek to ensnare, which he did who betrayed Him, as also those who crucified Him. Indeed, as for the fact that here too not just a bare statement is made, reading: *And they shall speak all that is evil against you,* but there is added, *untruly*; and again, *for my sake:* I think the addition is made with those in mind who would glory in being persecuted and defamed and would therefore say that Christ belonged to them because many evil things are said about them—when, in the first place, the things said are actually true if there is talk of their false belief; and again, even if occasionally also some false charges are broadcast, as often happens through the heedless talk of men, they are not therefore suffering this because of Christ. For he does not follow Christ who is not called a Christian in accordance with the true faith and the Catholic doctrine.

15. *Be glad and rejoice,* He said, *for your reward is great in heaven.* Here is not meant, I think, the higher parts of this visible universe; for our reward being of necessity in-

destructible and eternal, cannot be placed in things transitory and temporal. But " in heaven " means, I think, " in the spiritual firmament " where dwells everlasting holiness. In comparison with that heaven, a sinful soul is called " earth "; for to it when it sinned there was said: *Earth thou art and unto earth thou shalt return.*[32] It was of this heaven that the Apostle spoke: *Our conversation is in heaven.*[33] Hence they already experience this reward who rejoice in spiritual goods, but after death they will be perfected in every respect when even *this mortal will put on immortality.*[34]

For so, He said, *they persecuted also the Prophets that were before you* (12). Here He used " persecution " in a general sense, including both evil speech and defamation of character; and He made a fine point in citing an example to support His exhortation, for those who speak the truth generally encounter persecution; and the Prophets of old failed not to proclaim the truth through any fear of persecution.

CHAPTER 6

The salt of the earth and the light of the world.

16. Most appositely, therefore, follows: *You are the salt of the earth* (13), showing that they are to be regarded as stupid who in their pursuit of temporal goods or in their fear of losing them lose eternal goods which cannot be given or taken away by men. *But if the salt lose its savor, wherewith shall it be salted* (13)? That is, if you through whom nations are to be seasoned—if I may use the expression—if through fear of temporal persecution you lose the kingdom of heaven, who will there be to root out error from you, since God has chosen you as the instruments to dissipate the errancy of

others? Therefore salt that has lost its savor *is good for nothing but to be cast out and trodden on by men* (13). Not, therefore, is the one who suffers persecution trodden on by men, but the one who loses his savor by fearing persecution. Nothing but the inferior can be trampled on; but he is not inferior, however much he endures in his body on earth, who yet in spirit is rooted in heaven.

17. *You are the light of the world* (14). As He said above, *the salt of the earth*, so now He says, *the light of the world*. For above, "earth" is not to be taken as meaning this earth which we tread with the feet of our body, but the men who inhabit the earth, or even sinners for the staying and healing of whose sores the Lord sent the Apostles as salt: so in this place "world" ought to be taken as meaning not sky and earth, but men who are in the world or who love the world, to enlighten whom the Apostles were sent.

A city seated on a mountain cannot be hid (14): that is, founded upon a singularly great holiness, which is signified by the very mountain whereon the Lord spoke.

Neither do men light a candle and put it under a bushel (15). What are we to think? that the expression "under a bushel" must mean only the hiding of a candle, as if it were said: "No man lights a candle and then hides it"? Or does the word "bushel" contain a suggestion of its own, that "to put a candle under a bushel" is this—to make more of body comforts than of the preaching of the truth; that, therefore, a person does not preach the truth because he fears he will thereby suffer annoyances in things physical and temporal? And the term "bushel" is appropriately used, either to designate the repayment of a measure—for each will receive back what he did in his body, as the Apostle says: *that there every man may receive what he hath done in the body;* [35]

and as if referring to this bushel measure it is said in another place: *With what measure you mete, it shall be measured to you again;* [86] or because temporal concerns, which are carried on in the body, are begun and transacted within a definite measure of time—which is perhaps the significance of the " bushel "—whereas the eternal and spiritual are constricted to no such limitations, *for God doth not give the Spirit by measure.* [87] Therefore a person puts his candle under a bushel when he dims and hides in temporal concerns the light of good teaching.

But (they put the candle) *upon a candlestick* (15): "upon a candlestick "—he does this who delivers his body to the ministry of God that the preaching of the truth hold pre-eminence and the service of the body be given the least consideration; yet through that very service of the body the higher teaching should blaze forth which through bodily functions, that is, through voice and tongue and other actions of the body, should seep into the learners in good works. It is upon a candlestick, therefore, that the Apostle puts his candle when he says: *I do not so fight as one beating the air; but I chastise my body and bring it into subjection, lest perhaps in preaching to others I myself should be found worthless.* [88] But when He says: *that it may shine to all that are in the house* (15), I think " house " means the habitation of men, that is, the world itself, because of what He said above: *You are the light of the world;* or if anyone is inclined to interpret " house " as the Church, this, too, makes sense.

CHAPTER 7

Praise for good works must redound to God's glory.

18. *So let your light shine before men,* He said, *that they
may see your good works and glorify your Father who is in
heaven* (16). If He were saying no more than *So let your
light shine before men that they may see your good works,*
He would seem to have set up the objective in the praise of
men, which hypocrites seek and those who aim at honors and
snatch at any empty glory. Against such it is said: *If I yet
pleased men, I should not be the servant of Christ;* [39] and
through the Prophet: *Who please men have been confounded, because God hath held them as nothing;* [40] and
again: *God hath broken the bones of those that please
men;* [41] and again the Apostle: *Let us not be made desirous
of vain glory;* [42] and again the same: *But let a man prove
himself and so he shall have glory in himself and not in
another.* [43] Therefore, He said not merely: *that they may see
your good works,* but He added: *and glorify your Father who
is in heaven;* so that the mere fact that one pleases men
through his good works should not set up the objective in
this that he pleases men; but he should direct this to the
praise of God, and for this reason please men, that God may
be glorified in him. For it becomes those who offer praise to
honor not men but God, as the Lord showed in the case of
the man who was carried, when the crowds, awe-struck by
His manifestation of power in curing the paralytic, as is
written in the Gospel—*feared and glorified God who had
given such power to men.* [44] Copying whom the Apostle Paul
says: *But they had heard only: " He who persecuted us in*

*times . past doth now preach the faith which once he im-
pugned "; and they glorified God in me.*[45]

19. Therefore, after He had exhorted His hearers to prepare themselves to endure any trial in the cause of truth and
righteousness and not to hide the good which they were about
to receive, but to learn with such good will so as to teach
others, not referring their own good works to their own praise,
but to the glory of God, He begins now to instruct and teach
them what they should teach, as though in their quest they
were saying: Here we are, determined to endure anything
for Thy name and not to hide Thy doctrine; but just what is
this thing which Thou forbiddest us to hide and for which
Thou dost bid us endure all things? Art Thou about to say
something contrary to the things that have been written in
the Law? No, He said; *for do not think that I am come to
destroy the Law or the Prophets; I am not come to destroy
but to fulfill (17).*

CHAPTER 8

Christ brought the Law to perfection.

20. In this statement there is a twofold content. We must
consider each in turn. In saying: *I am not come to destroy
the Law but to fulfill,* He states that He does this either by
supplementing its deficiencies or by carrying out its content.
Let us, then, consider first what I have put first. Now, one
who supplements deficiency certainly does not thereby destroy what he finds but rather strengthens it by bringing it to
perfection. Hence He goes on and says: *Amen, I say to you,
till heaven and earth pass, one jot or one tittle shall not pass*

of the Law till all be fulfilled (18). For while there are being brought to pass the things which are added to bring about perfection, much more do the things come to pass which were premised as a beginning. As to what He says: *one jot or one tittle shall not pass of the Law,* nothing else can be meant than a vigorous expression of perfection.[46] The words taken by themselves show it. For the " jot " is smaller than the rest of the characters; it is made by one stroke; and the " tittle " is some tiny sign at the top of it.[47] And by these words He shows that even the very least things conduce to the perfection of the Law. Then He adds immediately: *For he that shall break one of these least commandments and shall so teach men shall be called the least in the kingdom of heaven* (19). Therefore the least commandments are signified by the one jot and the one tittle. And therefore, *he that shall break and so teach*—that is, who teaches not in accordance with what he finds and reads, but according to what he breaks—*shall be called the least in the kingdom of heaven.* And perhaps for that reason he will not be in the kingdom of heaven at all, where only the great can be; *but he that shall do and teach thus*—that is, who shall not break, and teach according to what he does not break—*shall be called great in the kingdom of heaven* (19). If he will be called great in the kingdom of heaven, it follows that he is in the kingdom of heaven, whither are admitted the great. What follows touches this point.

CHAPTER 9

*The justice of the Pharisees and the perfection
taught by Christ. Degrees of sin.*

21. *For I tell you the unless your justice abound more
than that of the Scribes and Pharisees, you shall not enter the
kingdom of heaven* (20). That is, you will not enter the
kingdom of heaven unless you comply not only with the least
prescriptions of the Law with which a man begins, but also
those which I add, *who am not come to destroy the Law, but
to fulfill.*[48]

But you are saying to me: If, when a minute ago He was
speaking of those least commandments, He said that he is
called least in the kingdom of heaven who breaks one of
them and teaches in accordance with his non-compliance; and
he is called great who keeps them and so teaches, and from
the fact that he is already destined for the kingdom of heaven
because he is great, what need to add to these least prescriptions of the Law if he can be in the kingdom of heaven
because whoever keeps them and so teaches is great?

Well, that statement—*But he that shall so do and teach,
he shall be called great in the kingdom of heaven*—must be
taken in this sense, namely, not according to those least
precepts but according to those which I am about to mention.
And what are they? *That your justice,* He said, should
abound more than that of the Scribes and Pharisees; for unless it should so abound, *you shall not enter into the kingdom
of heaven.* Therefore, if one breaks those least precepts and
so teaches, he shall be called least; but if he keeps those least
precepts and so teaches them, it does not yet follow that he is

to be considered great and prepared for the kingdom of heaven. Still he is not least to the extent that he is who breaks them. But that he may be great and acceptable for the kingdom, he should do and teach as Christ here teaches—that is to say, his justice should *abound more than that of the Scribes and Pharisees.* The justice of the Pharisees is, that they should not kill; the justice of those who will enter into the kingdom of heaven, is, that they should not be wrathful without cause. The least, therefore, is, not to kill; and one who breaks that will be called least in the kingdom of heaven; but one who follows the injunction not to kill, is not instantly made great and prepared for the kingdom of heaven, though he does advance a step or so upward. He will be perfected, however, if in addition he is not angry without cause; and if he will observe this, he will be much further removed from being a murderer. Consequently he who teaches that we should not be angry does not break the law forbidding murder but rather fulfills it. Thus we keep from inflicting harm both outwardly when we do not kill and in our heart when we are not angry.

22. He said, then: *You have heard that it was said to them of old, " Thou shalt not kill," and whosoever shall kill shall be in danger of the judgment. But I say to you that every one whosoever is angry with his brother without cause* [49] *shall be in danger of the judgment. But whosoever shall say to his brother: " Raca," shall be in danger of the council; and whosoever shall say: " Thou fool," shall be in danger of hell-fire* (21 f.).

What difference is there between being " in danger of the judgment " and " in danger of the council " and " in danger of hell-fire "? Evidently this last implies the most severe and suggests that some gradations are posited from the lighter to the more serious until one comes to the fire of hell. And therefore, if it is a lighter matter to be in danger of the judgment than to be in danger of the council; and again a lighter matter to be in danger of the council than to be in danger of the fire of hell: then we must regard as less serious to be angry with a brother without cause than to say " Raca "; and again, as less serious to say " Raca " than to say " Thou fool." For the liability would not have grades save that the sins also were mentioned by grades.

23. But one word is employed here that is obscure: *raca* is neither Greek nor Latin; the others, however, are familiar in our speech. Now, some have sought to extract the meaning of this word from the Greek, thinking that a ragged person is termed *raca* because in Greek a rag is called *rákos*; although when they are asked to translate " ragged person " into Greek, they do not say *raca*. A Latin translator, then, could put *pannosus* [49a] where he put *raca* and so not use a word which does not exist in the Latin language and in the Greek is unusual. More probable, therefore, is what I heard from a Hebrew when I asked him about it; for he said that it is a word that does not signify anything in particular, but expresses the feelings of an indignant person. Interjections are what the grammarians call these particles of speech indicating that a person is wrought-up; as when a person in sorrow says " Alas! " or an angry one " Pshaw! " Words of the sort are peculiar to a given language and are not easily translated into another language; this is the reason that compelled both the Greek and the Latin translator to put down the word itself since he could not find how to translate it. [50]

24. Grades there are, therefore, in these sins, so that one first becomes angry and keeps the emotion he harbors to

himself; if then that disturbance within the angry person wrests from him a vocal sound not signifying anything but witnessing to the distraught condition of his soul by the very fact of the outburst striking the one who has made him angry: this is certainly more than if the rising anger were suppressed in silence. But if not only a sound of the angry person should be heard but also a word which marks out and signifies an unmistakable upbraiding of him against whom it is directed, who doubts about this being something more than if only a sound of anger were given forth? Hence in the first there is one thing, namely, anger only; in the second, two things: both anger and a sound signifying anger; in the third, three things: anger, a sound that signifies anger, and in the word itself the expression of a definite upbraiding.

Look now also at the three stages of the indictment—judgment, council, the hell of fire. For in judgment there is still an opportunity for defense; in council, however, though the matter of judgment also usually comes up, yet because the very distinction compels the admission of some difference here, it seems that it belongs to council to pass sentence. Here the question is not directly concerned with the guilty person himself—whether he should be condemned—but the judges confer among themselves as to the punishment that ought to be inflicted on the one concerning whom it is already established that he is to be punished. But the hell of fire has no condemnation that is in the balance, like judgment; nor the punishment of the one condemned, as council; in fact, in the hell of fire the condemnation and the punishment of the one condemned is settled.

It is seen, therefore, that there are certain grades in sins and in the liability to punishment; but how these are shown invisibly by the punishments of souls, who can say? Therefore, the point to pay attention to is: what a difference there is between the justice of the Pharisees and that greater justice which leads one into the kingdom of heaven; because, while to kill is a more serious thing than to revile by a word, in the one case [51] killing renders one liable to the judgment, but in the other, anger renders one liable to the judgment, and this is the lightest of the three sins; because there it is among men that they discuss the question of killing; but here, everything is committed to the divine judgment where the end of those condemned is the hell of fire.

But if anyone says that murder is punished with heavier severity in greater justice: then, if reviling is punished by the hell of fire, we cannot but gather that there are varieties of hells.

25. Indeed, in these three statements it is to be noted that some words are understood. For the first statement we have all the words necessary, so that nothing is understood. *Whosoever is angry,* He says, *with his brother without cause, shall be in danger of the judgment.* In the second, however, He says: *And whosoever shall say to his brother " Raca,"* there is understood " without cause " and so there is added: *shall be in danger of the council.* Now in the third, when He says: *And whosoever shall say " Thou fool,"* two things are understood: " to his brother " and " without cause." Whence this is justified, that the Apostle calls the Galatians fools [52] whom he even calls brothers; [53] for he did not do it without cause. Therefore in this instance " brother " is to be understood, because regarding an enemy it is stated later on how even he must be treated according to the greater justice.

CHAPTER 10

*The internal disposition must be rectified before
external acts of religion can have worth.*

26. Next follows here: *If therefore thou offer thy gift at
the altar and there thou remember that thy brother hath
anything against thee: leave there thy offering before the
altar and go, reconcile thyself first with thy brother and then
coming offer thy gift* (23 f.). From this surely it is apparent
that a brother was spoken of above, since the statement which
follows is connected by a conjunction that indicates its relationship to the earlier statement. He did not say: " If thou
offerest thy gift at the altar "; but He said: *If therefore thou
offer thy gift at the altar.* For if it is not lawful to be angry
with one's brother without cause or to say " Raca " or to say
" Thou fool," much less is it lawful to retain in mind anything that may turn anger into hatred. In the same direction
points, too, what is said in another place: *Let not the sun
go down upon your anger.*[54] Therefore, when about to bring
a gift to the altar—so we are instructed—if we remember that
a brother has anything against us, we should leave the gift
before the altar and go and be reconciled with the brother,
then come and offer the gift. Now, if this is taken literally,
perhaps some one may believe that it ought to be so done if
the brother is present. For it cannot be deferred too long,
considering that you are ordered to leave your gift before the
altar. If, therefore, it is in regard to an absent brother and,
as can happen, even one who is overseas that such thought
comes to your mind, it would be absurd to think that your

gift is to be left before the altar for you to offer to God only after land and seas have been traveled over. And so we are forced to have recourse altogether within the spiritual, so that this statement can be understood without involving absurdity.

27. And so we can conceive of the altar spiritually as being faith itself in the interior temple of God whose token is the visible altar. Whatever gift we offer to God, whether prophecy or doctrine or prayer or hymn or psalm and whatever other such spiritual gifts come to mind, it cannot be acceptable to God unless it is grounded on sincerity of faith and as though placed there fixed and immovable, so that what we speak may be complete and inviolate. For many heretics, not having an altar, that is, true faith, speak blasphemies instead of praise; that is to say, laden down with earthly views, they, as it were, cast forth their prayers to the ground.

In this also the intention of the offerer must be flawless. Wherefore, when we are about to offer any such thing in our heart, this means in God's interior temple, *for the temple of God is holy*, he said, *which you are*; [55] and *in the inward man Christ dwells by faith in your hearts*. [56] If we recall that a brother has anything against us, this means: we have harmed him in some way, for then he has something against us. We have something against him if he has harmed us; in which case there is no need to go to seek reconciliation, for you will not seek pardon from him who has done you an injury, but only forgive him as you desire to be forgiven by the Lord for the sins you yourself commit. Therefore we must go to seek reconciliation when we remember that perhaps in some way we have harmed a brother. You must not go with the feet of the body, but with a movement of the soul, to prostrate yourself in humble sentiment before the brother to whom you will run with thoughts of affection in the sight of Him to whom you are about to offer your gift. For thus, too, should he be present, you will be able to reconcile him through no simulated disposition and regain his friendship by asking his pardon if you have already done so before God—going to him with no leaden movement of the body but with the swift affection of love; and then, coming, that is, recalling your attention to what you started to do, you will offer your gift.

28. But who does this that not without cause he is angry with a brother or not without cause says " Raca " or not without cause calls him a fool—the positive doing of which things stamps a person as excessively proud; or if perchance he has lapsed in any of these respects, that he then in suppliant spirit asks pardon—for that is the one remedy: who does this save one that is not puffed up by the spirit of vain ostentation? *Blessed, therefore, are the poor in spirit, for theirs is the kingdom of heaven.*[57] But now let us see what follows.

CHAPTER 11

Paying the last farthing. The adversary toward whom we must be well-disposed.

29. *Be well-disposed,* He said, *towards thy adversary betimes whilst thou art in the way with him, lest perhaps the adversary deliver thee to the judge and the judge deliver thee to the officer and thou be cast into prison. Amen, I say to thee, thou shalt not go out from thence till thou repay the last farthing* (25 f.).

I know who the " judge " is: *For the Father doth not judge any man, but hath given all judgment to the Son.*[57a] I know who the officer is: *And the angels*, he says, *ministered to Him.*[58] And it is with the angels, we believe, that He will come to judge the living and the dead. I know what the "prison" is: clearly, those punishments of darkness which elsewhere He calls exterior [59]—for this reason, I believe, because the joy of the divine rewards is something internal in the soul itself or even something more intimately personal, if such can be imagined; and concerning this joy it is said to the well-deserving servant: *Enter thou into the joy of thy lord.*[60] Thus, too, in our civil procedure the one being cast into prison is sent forth from the council chamber or office of the judge.

30. Now, as to "paying the last farthing," it makes good sense to take this to mean that nothing is left unpunished; just as we commonly say "down to the last dregs" [61] when we wish to express something as fully carried out, with nothing remaining. Or it may be that the phrase "the last farthing" was to signify our earthly sins. For the earth is found to be the fourth part of the several elements of this universe and, in fact, the last, if you start from the sky and number air second and water third and earth fourth. Therefore it may seem proper to say that *till thou pay the last farthing* means "till thou dost atone for thy earthly sins." For it was this, too, that the sinner heard: *Earth thou art and unto earth thou shalt return.*[62]

But as to the phrase "till thou pay"—I wonder if it does not refer to that punishment which is called eternal. For whence is he to pay that debt where the chance is no longer given to repent and live a more upright life? Thus it may be that here is put *till thou pay* in the same sense as in that passage where it is said: *Sit Thou at my right hand until I put all Thy enemies under Thy feet,*[63] for when the enemies have been placed under His feet, He will not cease to sit at the right; or in that by the Apostle: *For He must reign until He hath put all His enemies under His feet,*[64] for when they have been put there, He will not cease to reign. Therefore, just as in that passage it is understood that He will always reign of whom it was said: *He must reign until He hath put the enemies under His feet,* since they will always be under His feet, so here it can be taken that he will never go out concerning whom it was said: *Thou shalt not go out from thence till thou pay the last farthing,* because he is forever paying the last farthing while he is suffering the everlasting punishments of his earthly sins. Nor do I wish to give myself the appearance of having said this to suppress a more thorough-going treatment of punishments for sins—how in Scripture they are called eternal; though by all means avoiding them should take precedence over knowing them.

31. But now let us see who is that adversary towards whom we are ordered to be well-disposed when we are with him in the way. It must be either the devil or man or the flesh or God or His law. But towards the devil I do not see how we may be commanded to be well-disposed, that is, to be of one heart or of one mind with him. For you see, some took the Greek word given here—*eunoón*—and translated it with "of one heart"; others with "of one mind";[65] but neither are we told to show the devil any good will—for where there is good will there is friendship, and no one will say that we are to enter upon a friendship with the devil; nor is it expedient to be of one heart with him against whom we have declared war by renouncing[66] him once for all and on conquering whom we shall be crowned; nor ought we now consent to him through whom, if we had not consented to

him, we would never have fallen into the miseries that are ours.

As for man, though we are told to have peace with all men so far as we can—and surely good will and concord and sympathy can here be understood: yet I fail to see how I can take it that we are being delivered to the judge by man where I understand Christ to be the judge before whose judgment seat we must all be manifested,[67] as the Apostle says. How, therefore, is he who like us will appear before the judge going to deliver us over to the judge? Or take the example of a person being delivered over to a judge for the reason that he has injured a man, without, however, the man who suffered the injury actually delivering him: it is a far more acceptable interpretation that the guilty person is handed over to the judge by the law itself against which he acted in harming the person. Moreover, if one has harmed a person by killing him, there will be no time to get into agreement with him; because in that case he is not with him in the way, that is, in this life. And yet he will not for this reason be deprived of a restoration, if he does penance and takes refuge with the sacrifice of a contrite heart in the mercy of Him who forgives the sins of those that turn to Him and who rejoices upon one doing penance more than upon ninety-nine just.[68]

Still less do I see how we can be told to be well-disposed to, or concordant or sympathetic with, the flesh. Rather it is the sinners who love the flesh and agree with it and share its passions; whereas those who keep the flesh in utter subjection do not give in to it, but make it give in to them.

32. Well, then, possibly it is God with whom we are told to be in agreement and to be well-disposed towards Him in order to be reconciled to Him from whom we have parted by

committing sin, so that God can be called our adversary. Whom God opposes—He is beyond question the adversary of them; for *God resisteth the proud and giveth grace to the humble;* [69] *Pride is the beginning of all sin;* [70] and, *The beginning of the pride of man is to fall off from God.* [71] And the Apostle says: *For if, when we were enemies, we were reconciled to God by the death of His Son, much more, being reconciled, shall we be saved by His life.* [72] From which we can gather that no nature is an evil nature hostile to God, since those who were indeed enemies are reconciled to Him. Whoever, therefore, in this way, that is, in this life, will not be reconciled to God through the death of His Son, will be handed over to the judge by Him, because *the Father doth not judge any man; but hath given all judgment to the Son.* [73] This being so, all that I have so far treated in this section stands established.

There is only one point that raises a difficulty in this interpretation: How can it properly be said that we are in the way with God, if in this place He is to be taken as the adversary of the wicked with whom we are told to be reconciled *betimes?* The ubiquity of God may be the answer. As long as we are in the way we are unquestionably with Him. For, *if I ascend into heaven,* he said, *Thou art there; if I descend into hell, Thou art present; if I take my wings in a straight course and dwell in the uttermost parts of the sea, even there also shall Thy hand lead me and Thy right hand shall hold me.* [74]

Or if it is found objectionable to say that the wicked are with God—though there is no place where God is not—just as we do not say that the blind are with the light though the light is all about their eyes, then only one answer is left: that here we understand the adversary to be the commandment of God. For what adversary is there of those who wish to sin as great as the commandment of God, that is, His law and Divine Scripture, which were given us for this life, to be with us in the way? These we must not transgress if we do not want to be handed over to the Judge. With these we ought to be *at agreement betimes,* for no one knows when he is going to leave this life.

Now, who agrees with Divine Scripture save the one who religiously reads or hears it, according it the highest authority in that what he learns there does not make him hate because it thwarts his sinning? Rather, it makes him love what corrects him and makes him rejoice that his diseases receive attention until they are cured; and if he finds anything obscure or what appears to him absurd, he does not forthwith start a contest of contradicting but he prays for further knowledge and he bears in mind the reverence and good disposition of soul that is to be shown so commanding an authority. But who is the one who does this save one who sets out to uncover and know the will of the Father—not bristling with desire to object, but in a spirit made meek through loyalty? Therefore, *Blessed are the meek, for they shall possess the land.*

Now let us see what follows.

CHAPTER 12

Adultery. The three steps to sin. Habitual sin.

33. *You have heard that it was said to them of old: "Thou shalt not commit adultery." But I say to you that whosoever shall look on a woman to lust after her hath already committed adultery with her in his heart* (27 f.).

The lower morality is, not to commit adultery by union of bodies; but the higher morality of the kingdom of God is, not to commit adultery in the heart. Now, whoever does not commit adultery in his heart will all the more easily keep himself from physical adultery. He invigorated the lower morality who prescribed the higher; for He *came not to destroy the law but to fulfill.*

We should indeed reflect upon the fact that He did not say " every one who covets a woman," but *who looks on a woman to lust after her*, that is, directs his attention to her with this purpose in his mind, to lust after her. Now, this is not merely to be tickled [75] by the pleasure of the flesh, but it is the full consent to the pleasure: the forbidden craving is not checked, but, given the opportunity, it would gratify its desire.

34. For there are three steps in the commission of sin: suggestion, pleasure, consent. Suggestion comes about either through memory or a sense perception as when we see, hear, smell, taste or touch anything. If to enjoy any of these sensations brings pleasure, the pleasure, if forbidden, must be checked. For example, when we see food at a time when we are fasting, an appetite rises in the palate: that comes about only through pleasure; but on this occasion we do not fall in with the pleasure; we check it under the sway of reason. Were we to yield consent to it, we would commit sin surely, a sin in the heart known to God, though actually it may remain unknown to man.

Thus, then, there are these steps: the suggestion is made, as it were, by a serpent—that is, by a fleeting, swift and therefore momentary motion of bodies. For even though any such phantasms are within, within the soul, it is from the body, from without, that they are derived. And if any hidden emotion of the body apart from the five senses touches the soul, that, too, is momentary and swift; and the more stealthily it insinuates itself to thought, the more apposite the comparison with a serpent.

Therefore these three steps, as I began to say, are like that event recorded in Genesis: [76] a suggestion and a measure of suasion come about as if through a serpent; with the carnal appetite, as in Eve, there comes pleasure; and in reason, as was the case in the man, consent. When these become fact, man is, as it were, driven from Paradise, that is, from the most blessed light of innocence, into death—and most justly so. For he who uses suasion does not compel. And all natures in their order are beautiful in their gradation; but from the higher, among which the human soul has been placed, there must be no declining to a lower. Nor is anyone forced to do this; and therefore if he does it, he is punished by a just law of God; for not without his consent did he do it. But certainly before a habit has been formed [77] either there is no pleasure or it is so slight that there is hardly any. But to yield consent to a forbidden pleasure is a great sin; and the sin which a person commits in yielding consent is in his heart. If he goes further and puts this into action, his passion appears to be sated and quenched; but later on when the suggestion is repeated, there is enkindled a more intense pleasure; though this pleasure is still much less formidable than the pleasure that comes when repeated acts have formed a habit. To overcome a habit is most difficult. Yet one will overcome even a habit if he does not give up and does not dread a Christian's warfare against it under Him who is his leader and helper. And thus in a return to the wonted peace and order the husband is subjected to Christ and the wife to her husband. [78]

35. As, therefore, one comes to sin by three steps—suggestion, pleasure, consent—so there are three varieties of sin itself: in the heart, in the act, in the habit. This is like three aspects of death: one, so to speak, in the house, that is, when in the heart consent is given to lust; a second, with the corpse, as it were, already carried out through the door—when assent advances to action; a third when through force of habit the soul is, as it were, burdened down by a great weight—the rotting, so to speak, in the grave. That the Lord brought back to life souls from these three stages of death anyone will recognize who reads the Gospel. And perchance he will reflect upon the different types as indicated by the very words of Him who restores life: on one occasion He says: *Damsel, arise;* [79] elsewhere: *Young man, I say to thee: Arise;* [80] on another occasion: *He groaned in the spirit and wept* . . . ; and *again He groaned* . . . ; and then afterwards *He cried out with a loud voice: " Lazarus, come forth."* [81]

36. Wherefore by the name of adulterers who are mentioned in this section ought to be understood every carnal and lustful concupiscence. For since Scripture so constantly calls idolatry fornication, [82] and the Apostle Paul calls avarice by the name of idolatry, [83] who can doubt that every evil concupiscence is rightly called fornication, since the soul disregards the higher law by which it is ruled and prostitutes itself as for a price through base delight in lower natures and so completes its corruption?

Whoever, therefore, perceives some carnal pleasure rising in rebellion against his better desire through habit of sin, and that if it is not checked it will use violence and drag him into captivity, let him recollect as best he can what peace he has lost by sinning and let him cry out: *Unhappy man that I am, who shall deliver me from the body of this death? The grace of God, by Jesus Christ.*[84] When he thus cries out that he is unhappy, by his grief he is imploring the help of the Consoler. Nor is this merely a slight approach to blessedness, this recognition of unhappiness; and so again, *Blessed are the mourners, for they shall be comforted.*

CHAPTER 13

Scandal through the right eye and the right hand.

37. Then He goes on to say: *And if thy right eye scandalize thee, pluck it out and cast it from thee. For it is expedient for thee that one of thy members should perish, rather than that thy whole body go into hell* (29).[85]

Here there is need of heroic courage in order to cut off one's members. Whatever may be meant by an " eye," it unquestionably stands for something very highly treasured. For, too, when people wish to give strong expression to their affection, they will say: " I love him as my own eyes " or even " more than my own eyes." [86] And the addition of the word " right " serves perhaps to emphasize the intensity of affection. For, though in order to see, these eyes of ours are turned to their object at the same time and if both are turned they have equal power, yet men are more concerned over losing their right eye. Hence this seems to be the sense: Whatever it is which you so love that you rate it with your right eye—*if it scandalize thee*—that is, if it blocks your road to true happiness, tear it out and cast it from yourself. *For it is expedient for thee that one* of those things *should perish* that thou lovest as if they were fixed members of thee, *rather than that thy whole body go into hell.*

38. But since He follows with a similar statement con-cering the right hand: *If thy right hand scandalize thee, cut it off and cast it from thee. For it is expedient for thee that one of thy members should perish, rather than that thy whole body go into hell* (30), this compels us to look more closely into what He has spoken of as an " eye." The most significant notion suggested to me in this enquiry is that of a most beloved friend; for this assuredly is something which we can rightly call a member which we love very much; and he is a counsellor because he is an eye showing the way, as it were; and that in things divine because he is a right eye. Thus the left eye is indeed a beloved counsellor, but only in things earthly, pertaining to the necessities of the body. About scandal arising from this source it was superfluous to speak, since in such a case even the right eye is not to be spared. But in matters pertaining to divine things the coun-sellor becomes a source of scandal if under the name of religion and doctrine he tries to lead one to some baneful heresy. Therefore also the right hand should be taken as a beloved helper and attendant in divine works; for as we understand the eye to represent contemplation, so by the hand we rightly understand action. And this leaves us to understand by the left hand such activity as is necessary for this life and for our body.

CHAPTER 14

Marriage in the Old Law and in the New.

39. *And it hath been said, "Whosoever shall put away his wife, let him give her a bill of divorce"* (31).[87] This is the lower morality of the Pharisees, to which is not contrary what the Lord said: *But I say to you that whosoever shall put away his wife, excepting for the cause of fornication, maketh her to commit adultery; and he that shall marry her that is loosed by her husband committeth adultery* (32). For He who commanded a bill of divorce to be given [88] did not command that the wife be put away, but He said: *Whosoever shall put her away, let him give her a bill of divorce,* that the thought of the bill might temper the rash anger of him who has in mind to put out his wife. Therefore, He who sought delay in divorce signified as best He could to unfeeling men that He did not wish separation. And so the Lord Himself in another place, when asked about this, replied as follows: *Moses by reason of the hardness of your heart did this.*[89] For however hard-hearted he might be who would wish to put away his wife, yet when he would think of the bill of divorce and that by giving it he gave his wife the chance freely to marry another man, he would readily be reconciled. Therefore the Lord, to strengthen the rule that a wife should not lightly be put away, excepted only the case of fornication. All the rest of whatever annoyance might exist He orders to be courageously put up with in the interests of conjugal loyalty and chastity; and He calls by the name of adulterer even the man who marries a woman that has been separated from her husband.

Of this state the Apostle Paul points out the terminating point when he says that it must be maintained as long as the husband lives; but if he dies, he says, the woman may marry.[90] For he, too, maintained this rule and showed that this was not merely his advice, as in many a teaching, but a precept of the Lord who had laid down the law, when he said: *But to them that are married, not I but the Lord commandeth that the wife depart not from her husband; and if she depart, that she remain unmarried or be reconciled to her husband. And let not the husband put away his wife.*[91] I think that under a like form he would enjoin on the man that he is not to remarry if he has divorced his wife, or that he is to be reconciled to her. For it can come about that he should divorce his wife for the cause of fornication, which the Lord wished to be excepted. But now, if neither she is allowed to marry while her husband whom she has left is still alive nor is he allowed to remarry while his divorced wife is still alive, much less is it permitted to have illicit relations promiscuously.

More blessed surely are those marriages to be regarded which, whether after they were attended with the procreation of children or whether in them this earthly offspring has not even been considered, have been able to preserve continency with mutual consent between the parties; and this because nothing is done contrary to the precept wherein the Lord forbids putting away a wife; for he does not put away his wife who lives with her not carnally, but spiritually. Moreover, what is said by the Apostle is also observed: *It remaineth that they who have wives be as if they had none.*[92]

CHAPTER 15

Love and hatred of temporal relationships.

40. This fact more commonly perplexes the mind of the *little ones*,[93] who are however most eager to live according to Christ's precepts, that in another place the Lord Himself says: *Whosoever comes to me, and hates not his father and mother and wife and children and brethren and sisters and his own life besides, he cannot be my disciple.*[94] To the less intelligent this can seem a contradiction, because in the one instance He forbids putting away a wife except it be for the cause of fornication, but elsewhere He says that no one can be His disciple who does not hate his wife.

Now, if He were referring to the marriage act, He would not put father and mother and brothers in the same category. But how true it is that *the kingdom of heaven suffereth violence and the violent bear it away!* [95] Yes, what a need of violence there is that a man may love his enemies and hate his father and mother and wife and children and brethren! For He who calls to the kingdom of heaven commands both. And how these things do not contradict each other is easy to show with Him guiding us. Still, when these things are reconciled in thought, it is not easy to live them. Still again, it is most easy with the same One's assistance. For the eternal kingdom whither Christ has deigned to call His disciples, whom He also calls brothers,[96] does not have temporal necessities of the sort. For *there is neither Jew nor Greek, neither male nor female, neither bond nor free; but Christ is all and in all.*[97] And the Lord Himself said: *In the resurrection they shall neither marry nor be married, but shall be as the angels of God in heaven.*[98] Whoever, therefore, wishes here on earth to prepare for that kingdom of heaven, should hate not people as such, but those earthly necessities on which is built this life which is transitory and which is compassed by being born and dying. Whoever does not hate this does not yet love that life where there will be no destiny of being born and dying—the joiner of earthly wedlock.

41. Therefore, if I were to ask any good Christian who has a wife and though he is still having children with her, whether he would wish to have a wife in that kingdom: mindful in any case of the promise of God and mindful of that life where *this corruptible shall put on incorruption and this mortal shall put on immortality,*[99] though hesitating still by reason of his great love or at least by some love, he would answer with solemn protestation that most certainly he would not. Again, should I ask him if he would like to have his wife live with him after the resurrection when she has undergone the angelic change which is promised to the Saints,[100] he would wish her to live with him; and his affirmation of it will be as forceful as his previous denial. Thus it is characteristic of a good Christian to love in one woman the creature of God whom he desires to be transformed and renewed, but to hate corruptible and mortal intimacy and copulation—that is, to love the human being in her but to hate that which makes her a wife. Thus, too, he loves his enemy, not insomuch as he is an enemy but inasmuch as he is a human being; and hence he would wish the same to happen to his enemy as to himself, that is, to come into the kingdom of heaven restored and renewed.

The same is to be understood for father and mother and the other ties of blood, that in them we hate the lot of humankind to be born and to die,[101] while loving what can be taken with us to that kingdom where no one says "my father," but all say *our Father* [102] to the one God; not "my mother," but all say *our Mother* to *that Jerusalem;* [103] not "my brother," but "our brother" indifferently to all. Yes, our marriage with Him, once we have all been brought into one will be as to one spouse [104] who by the shedding of His blood freed us from the prostitution of this world. The disciple of Christ, therefore, must hate the transient in them whom he wants to come with him into the everlasting. And this hatred will be in proportion to his love of them.

42. A Christian, therefore, is free to live with a wife in concord: whether providing with her for a carnal want which the Apostle speaks of as *by indulgence, not by commandment,* [105] or for the propagation of children, and indeed this can to a degree be praiseworthy; or for a brother-sister companionship without any mingling of bodies, *having a wife as if he had none* [106]—which in Christian wedlock is most excellent and sublime—yet so as to hate in her everything that has to do with temporal necessity and to love the hope of everlasting blessedness. For unquestionably we hate what we wish would at some time not exist, like the very life of this world, which if we did not hate as being temporal we would not desire the future which has nothing to do with time. It is indeed this present life which is substituted for the soul, concerning which it is said in the passage mentioned: *He who hateth not . . . his own life besides, he cannot be my disciple.* [107] This life it is for which corruptible food is a necessity, regarding which food the Lord Himself said: *Is not the life more than the meat?* [108]—meaning this present life, for which food is a necessity. Again, when He says that He lays down His life for His sheep, [109] He surely means this

present life, declaring as He does that He is going to die for us.

CHAPTER 16

*Fornication as a ground for separation in marriage.
The case of a non-Christian spouse. Does
Christian marriage ever suffer the admis-
sion of a third party?*

43. Here arises another question: when the Lord permits the putting-away of a wife because of fornication, how is fornication to be taken in this passage? Is it as all understand it, namely, that we believe that to have been termed fornication which consists in the committing of lewd acts; or, as the Scriptures are wont to call fornication, as was said above, all forbidden depravity, such as idolatry or avarice and therefore every transgression of the law because of unlawful concupiscence? [110]

But let us see what the Apostle has, so that we may not say things unadvisedly; he says: *To them that are married, not I but the Lord commandeth that the wife depart not from her husband; and if she depart, that she remain unmarried or be reconciled to her husband.*[111] Evidently it can happen that the wife leaves her husband for the reason which the Lord approves as licit.

Or if the woman put away her husband for other reasons than fornication and the husband may not, what shall we say of his later statement: *And let not the husband put away his wife?* [112] Why did he not add what the Lord permits—*except for fornication*—unless because he wanted the same norm to be understood: that if the husband put her away—

a thing permitted in the case of fornication—he should remain without a wife or be reconciled to her? Indeed, reconciliation would not have been a bad thing for the husband of that woman to whom, when no one dared to stone her, the Lord said: *Go, and now make sure not to sin anymore.*[113] For He who said it is not lawful to put away a wife except for the cause of fornication also requires that the wife be kept if there is no charge of fornication against her; if such a charge does exist, He does not require a dismissal but merely allows it. In effect, what is said is this: Let it not be lawful for a woman to remarry except her husband has died; if she marry before her husband's death, she is guilty; if she does not marry after her husband's death, she is not guilty; for she was not commanded to remarry, but merely permitted to do so.

If, therefore, the norm governing these marriage rights is the same for man and woman, and this to such an extent that the same Apostle did not only say regarding the woman: *The wife hath not power of her own body, but the husband,* but did not pass him over, saying: *And in like manner the husband also hath not power of his own body, but the wife;*[114] if, then, as I said, the norm is the same, it ought to be understood that the woman is no more allowed to put away her husband except for the cause of fornication than it is allowed for him to put her away.

44. So we must consider what is to be our interpretation of fornication; and for this we must consult the Apostle, as we set out to do. He goes on to say: *But to the rest I speak, not the Lord.*[115] Here we must first enquire who are "the rest." In his earlier words he was speaking in the person of the Lord to those who are married; but now in his own person he speaks to the rest. Perhaps these are the unmarried. But

no; that does not follow, for he continues thus: *If any brother hath a wife that believeth not and she consent to dwell with him, let him not put her away.*[116] Therefore he is still addressing the married. What, then, is the meaning of " the rest " save that earlier he was speaking to those married persons who were both Christians, but now he is addressing the rest, that is, those not so married, where not both are believers?

And what does he say to them? *If any brother hath a wife that believeth not and she consent to dwell with him, let him not put her away. And if any woman hath a husband that believeth not and he consent to dwell with her, let her not put away her husband.*[117] If, therefore, he is not laying down a command in the Lord's name but is on his own authority giving a piece of advice, he is not a transgressor of a precept. It is the same as in what he says a little later concerning virgins that he has for them no precept of the Lord but is giving his own advice.[118] And his praise of virginity is so worded that he would have one who is so inclined to accept it with enthusiasm; yet if the person does not do this, he or she should not be judged to have gone against the law. For it is one thing that is commanded, another that is advised, another that is conceded. A woman is commanded not to depart from her husband; if she depart, to remain unmarried or be reconciled to her husband. She cannot, therefore, licitly do otherwise. A Christian husband is advised if he have an infidel wife and she consent to remain married to him, not to put her away. He can, therefore, licitly put her away, for it is not the Lord's command not to do so but only the advice of the Apostle. It is the same as when an unmarried woman is advised not to marry: if she marry, she is not taking the advice, it is true, but she is not going against a command. A concession is implied in his words: *But I speak this by indulgence, not by commandment.*[119]

Wherefore, if it is allowed to put away a non-Christian spouse—though it is better not to—and yet it is not allowed by the Lord's law to put away a spouse except for the cause of fornication: then unbelief itself is likewise fornication.

45. My dear Apostle, what is this you are saying? Surely, that a believing husband should not put away an unbelieving woman who consents to dwell with him.

Yes, he says.

Now, then, seeing that the Lord commands that a husband is not to put away his wife except because of fornication, why do you in this instance say, *I speak, not the Lord?*

Evidently because idolatry which unbelievers practise and any other corrupting superstition is fornication.

The Lord gave permission to put away a wife if she is guilty of fornication; but because He permitted it and did not order it, He gave His Apostle an opportunity to advise a husband inclined to put away his unbelieving wife not to do so, with the possible result that she may thus become a believer. *For,* he says, *the unbelieving husband is sanctified in his wife; and the unbelieving wife is sanctified in the brother.*[120] I take it that it already had come to pass that not a few women through the influence of their believing husbands and men through the influence of their believing wives were embracing the faith, and Paul was exhorting others by these examples without mentioning names to support his advice. Then follows: *otherwise your children should be unclean; but now they are holy.*[121] For already there were Christian children who at the instance of one of the parents or by consent of both had been sanctified.[122] This would not have been the case unless there had been a division of sentiment in the marriage union by one of the parties becoming a Christian and if the unbelief of the spouse had not been borne with until in due season belief should come. This, I believe, was in the mind of Him to whom I would ascribe the words: *If thou shalt spend anything over and above, I at my return will repay thee.*[123]

46. Further, if unbelief is fornication and idolatry is unbelief and avarice is idolatry, there can be no question but that avarice is fornication. If, then, avarice is fornication, who can rightly keep from the category of fornication any illicit concupiscences whatever? From this we gather that because of illicit concupiscences, not only those which take place in adulterous acts with another's husband or wife, but any illicit concupiscences whatever that bring the soul to an improper use of the body and so cause it to stray from the law of God and to be corrupted to its ruin and shame, a husband can without grave sin put away his wife and a wife her husband; for the Lord makes the cause of fornication an exception; and here fornication, as we considered above, must be understood by us in a general and universal sense.[124]

47. But when He says, *except for the cause of fornication,* He did not state of which of them—the man or the woman. For not only is it permitted to put away a wife guilty of fornication but whoever also puts away his wife because she is trying to force him into fornication, certainly such a one is putting away his wife because of fornication. For example, a man is urged by his wife to sacrifice to idols: if he puts away such a person, he does so because of fornication, not only on her part, but on his also; on her part, because she commits fornication; on his part, to keep from committing fornication.

But nothing is more wicked than to put away a wife for the cause of fornication if at the same time he himself is guilty of fornication. For that passage confronts him: *For wherein thou judgest another, thou condemnest thyself. For thou dost the same things which thou judgest.*[125] Hence, whoever wishes to put away his wife for the cause of fornication should himself antecedently be clear of a like charge; and I would say the same for a woman.

48. And as to what He says: *He that shall marry her that is loosed from her husband committeth adultery,* the question can be raised, whether she also who is married commits adultery in the same way as he does who marries her. She, too, let us note, is commanded to remain unmarried or be reconciled to her husband; this, however, as is stated, on the supposition that she leaves her husband. It makes a great difference whether she puts away or is put away. For if she puts away her husband and marries another, she appears, by her wish to change the marriage, to have left her former husband; and without any doubt such thinking constitutes adultery. Whereas if she is put away by her husband with whom it is her wish to remain, the man who marries her is guilty of adultery according to the words of the Lord; but whether or not she herself is answerable for a like crime is uncertain. Still, it would seem much harder to explain how when man and woman with equal consent enter into conjugal relations one of them should be an adulterer and the other not. And also the consideration that if the man commits adultery by marrying her who has been put away by her husband—granting that she did not put away but was put away—she on her part causes him to commit adultery, which is no less forbidden by the Lord. The conclusion, therefore, is that whether the husband puts her away or she puts away

her husband, she must remain unmarried or be reconciled to her husband.[125a]

49. Again a question comes: suppose a wife who is barren or unwilling to submit to the marital act: is it possible for the husband with her permission to use another woman—not the wife of another nor one put away by her husband—without committing the sin of fornication? In the history of the Old Testament, it is true, an example of this is found.[126] But now greater commandments are in force to which the human race came once it had passed that stage. These former things should be treated in the light of the ages that must be distinguished in the dispensation of Divine Providence which came to the aid of mankind in a most perfectly ordered way;[127] but they cannot be followed as a rule of life.

But yet whether the words of the Apostle: *The wife hath not power of her own body, but the husband; and in like manner the husband also hath not power of his own body, but the wife,*[128] can bear the construction that with his wife's permission, who has the power of her husband's body, her husband can have intercourse with another woman who is not the wife of another nor separated from her husband: no, such a supposition must not be made; otherwise it would appear that with her husband's consent a woman could do this too—a thing which the universal moral sense rejects.

50. And yet some cases can happen where it might appear that a wife also, with her husband's consent, would be obligated to do this for the sake of her husband himself. Such a thing is said to have happened at Antioch about fifty years ago in the times of Constantius.

Acindynus[129] was then governor, a man who was also of consular rank. When he demanded of a man the payment of a pound of gold owed to the imperial treasury, acting upon I do not know what motive, he did a thing which is very often fraught with danger in those public officials to whom anything and everything is allowed, or rather, is thought by them to be allowed: he threatened with oaths and stormy language to put the man to death if he did not pay the aforesaid gold by a certain date which he had fixed. And so as he was kept in harsh confinement and he was unable to rid himself of the debt, the dread day began to draw ominously near.

Now, he happened to have a very beautiful wife; but she was without money to come to her husband's aid. When a certain wealthy man, infatuated by the woman's beauty, had learned of her husband's plight, he sent her word that he would give her a pound of gold if for a single night she would agree to have intercourse with him. Whereupon, knowing that not she had power over her own body, but her husband, she reported back to him that for her husband's sake she was ready to comply, provided her husband, the conjugal master of her body to whom all her chastity was owed, decided—thus disposing of a matter properly his own— that for his life's sake this should be done. He was grateful and told her to do this; not at all deeming the intercourse to be adultery because there was no lust on her part, and again her great love for her husband demanded it, at his own bidding and will. The woman went to the mansion of the rich man, did what the lecher wished; but she gave her body only to her husband, who was asking not, as at other times, to lie with her but to live. She received the gold; but he who gave it, surreptitiously took back what he had given and substituted a duplicate bag with earth in it. When the woman discovered it, she was already back at her home. She rushed into the street to publish aloud what she had done, animated by the same tender affection for her husband by which she had been driven to do it. She protests to the governor, tells him the whole story, shows how she has been victimized. And then the governor first pronounces himself guilty because by his threats it had come to this, and, as if passing sentence on another, decides that " a pound of gold should be paid into the imperial treasury from the property of Acindynus "; but that the woman should be installed as the mistress of the piece of land whence she had received earth in place of gold.

Out of this story I make no argument of any sort. Let each one pass judgment as he wishes. The account is taken from no divine sources. But when the incident is told, man's moral sense is not so ready to condemn what happened in this woman's case at the behest of her husband, as we were shocked before when the case itself was being suggested without any illustration.

However, in this part of the Gospel nothing is to be noted with closer attention than that fornication is so great an evil that, while in wedlock people are bound to each other by so strong a bond, this one reason for breaking it is excepted; and what fornication is we have already seen.

CHAPTER 17

Swearing.

51. *Again*, He said, *you have heard that it was said to them of old, " Thou shalt not forswear thyself, but thou shalt perform thy oath to the Lord."* [130] *But I say to you, not to swear at all, neither by heaven, for it is the throne of God; nor by the earth, for it is His footstool; nor by Jerusalem, for*

it is the city of the great king. Neither shalt thou swear by thy head, because thou canst not make one hair white or black. But let your speech be: Yes, Yes—No, No. And that which is over and above is of evil (33-37).

The righteousness of the Pharisees is not to commit perjury. This righteousness He supports who forbids swearing with regard to the righteousness of the kingdom of heaven. For as one who does not speak at all cannot speak what is false, so one who does not swear cannot swear falsely. Yet, since he swears who calls God to witness, we must make earnest study of this section, or the Apostle may seem to have acted in opposition to the Lord's precept. He often swore in this manner, when he says: *Now the things which I write to you, behold, before God, I lie not;* [131] and again: *The God and Father of our Lord Jesus Christ, who is blessed forever, knoweth that I lie not.* [132] Such, too, is this: *For God is my witness, whom I serve in my spirit in the gospel of His Son, that without ceasing I make commemoration of you always in my prayers.* [133]

Or perhaps someone will say that we have swearing only when the word " by " is expressed with the object by which we swear; so that he did not swear because he did not say " by God," but said *God is my witness.* To have this notion is ridiculous; yet because of quibblers and slow-witted persons, to keep anyone from thinking that there is a difference, let him know that the Apostle has sworn in this manner, saying: *I die daily, I protest by your glory.* [134] And lest anyone think that what is said here is the same as saying, " your glory makes me die daily "—as when we say " by his teaching he became learned," meaning thereby that *through* his teaching it came about that he was perfectly instructed: this is settled by the Greek manuscripts which read: *Nē tēn kaú-*

chēsin hymetéran—a formula used only by one taking an oath.[135]

So, then, it is seen that the Lord's command not to swear was given that a person might not run into using oaths as something good, and by his readiness to swear because of the habit, lapse into false swearing. Wherefore let one who realizes that swearing is to be accounted not among the better things but the necessary ones, refrain, as much as possible, from resorting to it; necessity alone should be the exception, when he sees persons reluctant to believe something which they would do well to believe, unless they are convinced by an oath. It is to this, then, that the statement applies: *Let your speech be Yes, Yes—No, No*; this is good and should be our ideal. *That which is over and above is of evil*—that is, if you are obliged to swear, realize that the necessity lies on you because of the weakness of those whom you are trying to convince; and this weakness is certainly an evil, one from which we daily pray to be delivered, when we say: *Deliver us from evil.*[136]

He did not, then, say: "that which is over and above is evil"; for you are not doing evil when you are making a proper use of an oath, which, though not properly good, is yet necessary to convince another for his good; but He said it *is of evil* on the part of him because of whose weakness you are compelled to swear.

But no one knows save through experience how difficult it is both to rid oneself of a habit of swearing and never to do without good reason what at times necessity forces one to do.[137]

52. Now, it may be asked why when it was said, *But I say to you, not to swear at all*, the addition was made: *neither by heaven, for it is the throne of God*, etc., down to *neither by*

thy head. I believe it was for this reason, that the Jews did not think themselves bound by an oath if they had sworn by any of these several things; and because they had heard, *Thou shalt perform thy oath to the Lord,* they did not think themselves obligated to the Lord by their oaths if they swore by heaven or earth or by Jerusalem or by their head. This happened not because of a defect in the Lawgiver but because they had misinterpreted the law.

The Lord, therefore, teaches that among the creatures of God nothing is so trivial that anyone should think that he can perjure himself by it; and this because created things, from the highest to the lowest, beginning with the throne of God and going down to a white or black hair, are ruled by Divine Providence. *Neither by heaven,* says He, *for it is the throne of God; nor by the earth, for it is His footstool:* that is, when you swear by heaven or earth, you are not to think that you are not held to perform your oaths to the Lord; for you are convicted of swearing by Him whose throne is heaven and whose footstool is the earth. *Neither by Jerusalem, for it is the city of the great king*—which is better stated than if He had said "my city," though it is to be taken that He meant this; and because He is the Lord, he must perform his oaths to the Lord who swears by Jerusalem. *Neither shalt thou swear by thy head:* and what can anyone imagine more his own than his head? Yet, how is it ours since we have no power to make a single hair white or black? Therefore anyone who wishes to swear even by his head is still bound to perform his oath to the Lord, ineffably controlling all things and everywhere present. And here all other things, too, are understood which it was of course impossible to enumerate— an example of which we mentioned in that saying of the Apostle: *I die daily, I protest by your glory.* To show that he was bound to perform this oath to the Lord, he added, *which I have in Christ Jesus.*

53. However—it is for some earthly-minded people that I say this—we are not to think that because heaven is called God's throne and the earth His footstool, therefore God has members arranged in heaven and on earth, like we have when we sit down. The throne of God stands for judgment. And since in the whole body of the universe heaven is the most beautiful in appearance and the earth the least, and the divine power, as it were, is more present where beauty excels, though yet disposing of the least of it in the farthest and lowest parts, He is said to sit in heaven and to tread upon the earth.

In a spiritual sense, however, the name heaven stands for holy souls and earth for sinful ones. Now, since *the spiritual man judgeth all things and himself is judged of no man,*[188] he is fitly called the seat of God. But because the sinner to whom it was said, *Earth thou art and unto earth thou shalt return* [139]—through justice giving award according to merit— is placed in the lowest rank and is punished under the law because he did not wish to stay within the law, he is properly taken as His footstool.

CHAPTER 18

Be a militant Christian!

54. Now, to conclude this summary, what more laborious effort can be mentioned or thought of, one in which the believing soul is called on to exercise industriously its every energy, than overcoming a bad habit? Let it cut off members

that prevent approach to the kingdom of heaven and not be smitten with grief for doing so. In the matter of conjugal fidelity let it bear everything which, however annoying it may be, is still above the reproach of illicit corruption, that is, fornication. For example, if one has a wife who is barren, deformed or feeble or blind or deaf or lame or anything else, or confined with diseases and pains and infirmities and whatever else may come to mind in the way of most dreadful things—fornication excepted: he is to endure all this in the cause of his conjugal fidelity and companionship. More, not only is he not to cast such a one from him but also if he does not have a wife, he is not to marry her who has been freed from her husband, though she be beautiful, healthy, rich, fruitful. And if it is not permitted to do these things, still less should he think it permissible for him to seek out any other forbidden relationship; and he must so flee from fornication as to withdraw himself from any shameful moral taint. Let him speak the truth and that with authority, not by the interlarding of oaths but by his upright living. Let him in the face of all the countless throngs of bad habits rising up in rebellion against him—and in order that all may be recognized, we have mentioned a few—betake himself to the citadel of Christian warfare [140] and from this vantage post, as it were, put them down.

But who would dare encounter such labors as these save him who is so enamored of what is right that he assails heaven by force, burning, so to speak, with a most vehement hunger and thirst and thinking that he has no life until his longing for that rightness is fulfilled? For in no way can he be strong enough to endure everything which in the rooting-up of bad habits the lovers of this world regard as toilsome and arduous and altogether too difficult. *Blessed, therefore, who hunger and thirst after justice, for they shall have their fill.*

55. But if one engaged in these efforts encounters difficulty, and, making his way by hard and painful efforts, encompassed with manifold temptations, and beholding the troubles of his past life surging up all around him, he fears that he cannot carry through his endeavors, let him put his mind to a plan for obtaining assistance. And what other plan is there but that he bear the infirmity of others and that he relieve it as much as he can, who himself wishes for divine assistance? And so, therefore, let us look at the precepts of mercy. The meek and the merciful seem to be one, but there is this difference: the meek, as I have already shown, in his love for God does not oppose the divine sentences directed against his sins nor those words of God which as yet he does not understand; but he confers no benefit upon him whom he does not contradict or resist; whereas the merciful person in offering no resistance does this for the amendment of him whom he would make worse by resisting.

CHAPTER 19

The suffering of wrongs as exemplified by Christ and St. Paul. Slavery.

56. The Lord therefore goes on and says: *You have heard that it hath been said, " An eye for an eye and a tooth for a tooth." But I say to you, not to resist evil, but if one strike thee on thy right cheek, turn to him also the other; and if a man will contend with thee in judgment and take away thy coat, let go thy garment* [141] *also unto him. And whosoever*

*will force thee one mile, go with him other two. Give to him
that asketh of thee, and from him that would borrow of thee
turn not away* (38-42).

The lower morality of the Pharisees is, not to exceed due
measure in revenge, not to pay back more than you have
received. And, really, this is a high level; for you do not
easily find a person content to return only blow for blow or
make only one reply to the word of the man scoffing at him,
and that just enough to match him. But he usually is less
moderate in avenging himself, whether perturbed by his
anger or because he deems it only just that one who comes
with insult should receive more of the same than he who
was not the insulter to begin with. This latter frame of mind
the Law in great part restrained, in which it was written:
An eye for an eye and a tooth for a tooth. By these words
moderation is indicated: revenge is not to exceed the wrong
done.[142] And this is the beginning of peace; but perfect peace
is to have no desire at all for such revenge.

57. Therefore between that first which is beyond the law,
that a greater evil be returned for a lesser evil, and that which
the Lord said to His disciples to carry out, that no evil whatever be returned for an evil received, this holds a middle
course, so to speak, that only so much be returned as was
given; and in the temporal economy [143] this represents a
transition from the highest discord to the highest concord.

See, therefore, what a distance separates an aggressor bent
on mischief and harm from him who does not retaliate even
when he has been harmed! Now, one who was not an aggressor but yet when harmed paid back—in fact or intention—
more than he received, has somewhat withdrawn from the
extreme of injustice and has drawn nearer to perfect justice;
however, he is not yet abiding by what the Mosaic Law

demands of him. The person, then, who pays back no more than he has received has already forgiven something. For he who wrongs another does not deserve merely what his victim has endured innocently.

Accordingly, this imperfect justice, one that is marked not by harshness but by mercy, He perfects who came to fulfill the Law, not to destroy it. He left implied two intervening lines of conduct and chose to speak of the highest phase— mercy. For there is still a choice of action for one who does not comply fully with the command that leads to the kingdom of heaven—not to make an even return, but less, for example, one blow for two, or to cut off an ear in retaliation for the plucking out of an eye. An advance over this is not to retaliate at all. This comes closer to observing the Lord's precept, but still it falls short of it. For the Lord this is still not enough, if for the evil received you pay back no evil unless you are ready to take on even more. Hence He does not say: " But I say to you not to return evil for evil," though this, too, would constitute a great precept, but He says *not to resist evil*, so that not only are you not to requite what may be inflicted on you, but you are not even to resist further inflictions. This is also what He illustrates in the following: *But if one strike thee on thy right cheek, turn to him also the other.* He does not say " If someone hits you, do not hit him back," but, " show yourself willing to receive another blow from him." And that this is of the nature of compassion, they particularly realize who wait on those whom they deeply love as if they were their children or very dear friends in sickness— the helpless little ones or the demented, from whom they often have much to endure; and if their welfare demands it, they show they are ready to put up with even more, until the debility of youth or disease has passed. As to those, therefore, whom the Lord, the Physician of souls,[144] was instructing how to devote themselves to their fellow men, what else could He teach them but calm endurance of the weakness of those whose welfare they had at heart? For, of course, all baseness springs from weakness of character; because nothing is more irreproachable than he who is made perfect in strength of character.

58. But it may be asked, what is meant by " the right cheek." So it is found in the Greek versions which are the more reliable, while many of the Latin texts have only " cheek," not " right cheek." Now, it is the face whereby a person is recognized. We read, moreover, in the Apostle: *For you suffer if a man bring you into bondage, if a man devour you, if a man take from you, if a man be lifted up, if a man strike you on the face*; and then he immediately subjoins, *I speak according to dishonor*,[145] meaning to explain what to be struck on the face is, namely, to be contemned and despised. This, unquestionably, the Apostle says not for this purpose, that they should not put up with such persons; it is rather himself he would have them bear with, who loved them so much that he was willing to be spent himself for them.[146]

But since we cannot speak of a right and left face and yet see a nobility in it both divine and human, we divide it into a right and a left cheek, so to speak, that if any disciple of Christ should have to suffer contempt because he is a Christian, he is all the more prepared to have that contempt directed towards him if he holds any honors of this world. Thus the same Apostle, if he had said nothing about the dignity which he possessed in the world when actually in his person men were persecuting the Christian name, he would not have turned the other cheek to those smiting his right cheek.

Indeed, by saying: *I am a Roman citizen*,[147] he did not show himself unwilling to have what he held as naught contemned in him by those who had despised in him a name so precious and so synonymous with salvation. And afterwards was he perhaps any less willing to bear chains which it was against the law to put on Roman citizens, or did he wish to accuse anyone for heaping this indignity on him? And if there were those who spared him because of his title to Roman citizenship, he did not therefore refrain from offering himself to be struck, desirous as he was by patient endurance to correct in their misdirection men whom he saw honoring in him the left rather than the right element.[148]

For that only need be considered: the spirit in which he did everything, how kind and gracious he was towards those who were making him suffer these things. When, for example, by the high priest's order he was also slapped, what appeared to have been spoken insolently in the words, *God will strike thee, thou whited wall*,[149] sounds like an insult to those who do not understand it; but to those who do, it is a prophecy. For a "whited wall" is hypocrisy, in this case pretense parading a priestly dignity and concealing under such title, as under a white covering, an inner and, to put it thus, filthy foulness. But as to humility's demands, these he kept in remarkable observance: when they said to him, *Dost thou revile the high priest?* he said: *I knew not, brethren, that he is the high priest. For it is written: "Thou shalt not speak evil of the prince of thy people."* [150] Here he showed with what poise of soul he had said what seemed to have been spoken in anger: his answer came so quickly and was so mildly phrased—a thing which no indignant or ruffled persons can do. And by that very fact he spoke the truth to those who understood aright: *I knew not that he is the high*

priest; which is as if he had said: " I know another High
Priest for whose name I bear such things, whom it is not
lawful to revile and whom you are reviling since in me it is
only His name that you hate."

So, one must not speak hypocritically about these matters,
but deep down in his heart be ready for whatever may come,
to say with the Prophet: *My heart is ready, O God, my
heart is ready.*[151] Many, it is true, know how to turn the other
cheek, but do not know how to love the person who strikes
them. Conversely, it is true that the Lord Himself, who
certainly was the first to fulfill the precepts which He taught,
did not offer the other cheek to the underling of the high
priest who was slapping Him, but said besides: *If I have
spoken evil, charge me with evil; if well, why strikest thou
me?*[152] But this does not mean that for the salvation of all
He was not ready in His heart not only to be struck on His
other cheek, but even to have His whole body crucified.

59. Therefore, too, what follows: *And if a man will contend with thee in judgment and take away thy coat, let go
thy garment also unto him,* is rightly understood as a precept
touching preparation of heart, not the actual doing of what is
said. And what is said about coat and garment applies not
to these things only, but to all things which we say we have
a right in this life to call our own. For if this has been commanded with regard to necessities, how much more becoming
is it to hold as naught things superfluous! But, as I was
saying, those things I have referred to as ours must be included in that generalization the Lord Himself uses when
He gives the precept, saying: *And if a man will contend with
thee in judgment and take away thy coat. . . .* Here, then,
we are to understand all such things for which we may be
brought into litigation, whereby they may pass from our

ownership to his who contends or in behalf of whom he contends—clothes, for instance, house, land, a beast of burden, and, in general, any kind of property.

But whether this is to apply to slaves also is a weighty problem.[153] For no Christian ought to possess a slave as he might a horse or money; and this, despite the fact that a horse might command a higher price than a slave and something in gold or silver a much higher price. But if that slave is receiving from you, his master, a better moral education and training, one that is more conducive to his worship of God,[154] than he can possibly receive from him who would take him away, I do not know if anyone would venture to say that he should be disregarded the same as a garment. For indeed it is man's duty to love man as he does himself, to whom the Master of all, as is shown in what follows, has given command to love even his enemies.

60. This is to be noted: every coat is a garment, but not every garment is a coat. Evidently, the term "garment" is more comprehensive than the term "coat"; and so I think the words were so put: *If a man will contend with thee in judgment and take away thy coat, let go thy garment also unto him*, as if He had said: "If a man wishes to take your coat, give him also whatever other article of clothes you have." For this reason some translators have used the word *pallium* for *himátion* in the Greek.[155]

61. *And whosoever will force thee one mile*, He says, *go with him other two*. And this, surely, not that you actually walk the two miles, but that you should be disposed to do so. For in the history of Christianity—in which is precedent— you will find nothing of the sort done by the Saints, or by the Lord Himself, though in His human nature which He deigned to assume He was giving us an example of how to

live; while, on the other hand, you may find them everywhere to have been ready to bear patiently whatever may have
been forced on them unreasonably.

But are we to think that *go with him other two* was said
merely by way of example? Or was it that He wished to
come to the number "three"—for that number signifies
perfection [155a]—so that everyone would remember when he
does this that he is practicing perfect righteousness by com-
passionately bearing with the infirmities of such as he wishes
restored to their senses? It appears possible that for this
reason too He introduced these precepts by three examples.
The first is, *If one strike thee on the cheek*; the second, *If a
man will take away thy coat*; the third, *If a man will force
thee one mile.* In this third example the double is added to
one to make three. And if in this instance this number does
not signify perfection, as has been set forth, then this may be
the sense, that what in the laying-down of His precepts, as it
were, took an easy enough start, gradually became more
formidable until it developed into the sufferance of twice as
much more. For, to begin with, He wished the other cheek
to be offered when the right cheek had been struck, so that
you would be prepared to endure less than you had already
endured. For whatever the right cheek signifies, it certainly
stands for something more dear than what is signified by the
left; and if one has been made to endure something in a
matter that means much to him, then, if he is called upon to
do the same in a matter of less consequence, it is something
less. Secondly, in the case of him who wishes to take away a
coat, He commands that the garment also should be turned
over to him; the value of which is the same or not much
greater, but not twice as great. In the third place, in regard
to the mile to which He says two should be added, He tells

you that you should bear with even twice as much more—
thus signifying that if a person wishes to be less mean towards
you than he has already been, or just as mean or more so,
you should put up with it with a calm mind.

CHAPTER 20

Fraternal correction. Giving and lending to others.

62. Certainly, in the comprehension of these three examples I see no class of indignity passed over. For every
indignity we are forced to suffer falls under one of two
classes: in the first, no restitution is possible; in the second,
this is possible. But in the former, where restitution is impossible, a common compensation is revenge. What, then,
comes of returning blow for blow? Is that which has been
harmed in the body thereby restored to its original state? It
is the conceited one who craves for palliatives of this sort.
But they bring no comfort to a strong and well man; on the
contrary, he judges it better to endure the weakness of
another in a spirit of compassion than to cater to his own
weakness—which does not exist—by inflicting punishment on
another.

63. And here there is no prohibition against punishment
aimed at correction; for this, too, is of the nature of mercy
and does not stop the way of that disposition by which one
proposes to be prepared to endure still more from him whom
he wishes to amend. But only he is competent to inflict this
sort of punishment who by the greatness of his love has
overcome the hatred with which those are wont to be inflamed
who desire to be avenged. For example, there is no reason

to fear that parents would appear to hate their little son if they whip him for committing a wrong, so that he may not do it again. And assuredly the perfection of love is proposed to us in our being asked to imitate God the Father Himself, when in the following words it is said: *Love your enemies, do good to them that hate you, and pray for them that persecute you* (44); and yet the Prophet speaks of Him in this way: *For whom the Lord loveth, He chastiseth, and He scourgeth every son whom He receiveth.*[156] The Lord, too, says: *The servant that knows not the will of his lord and does things worthy of stripes shall be beaten with few stripes; but the servant who knows the will of his lord and does things worthy of stripes shall be beaten with many stripes.*[157]

This, therefore, is all that is required: that he do the punishing who in the natural order of things is invested with power to do so, and that he punish with the benevolence of a father towards his young child, whom because of his youth he cannot yet hate. Clearly, from here we can draw the best example to show to satisfaction that wrongdoing can better be punished in a spirit of love than be left unpunished; that the one who punishes does not wish the one punished to be unhappy by the punishment but happy through the correction he receives; but at the same time he is ready, if need be, to put up calmly with further annoyance on the part of him whose improvement he desires, whether or not he is empowered to force him.

64. But great and holy men who, though knowing fully well that death which separates the soul from the body is nothing to be dreaded, nevertheless acted according to the mind of those who would fear it and punished a number of transgressions with death; and this because on the one hand a salutary fear was thereby instilled in the living, and on the

other, regarding those who were being punished by death, it was not death that could harm them, but sin which could grow if they were allowed to live. This was no rash conclusion on the part of those to whom God had given such a judgment. Hence it was that Elias put many to death with his own hand and with fire asked for from on high.[158] And many other great and God-inspired men have done this, without being rash—in a like spirit of providing for the best interests of humanity.

When the disciples had cited the example of this Elias, reminding the Lord of what had been done by him that He might give to them, too, the power of calling down fire from heaven to consume those who were refusing Him hospitality, the Lord reproved in them not the example of the holy Prophet but the ignorance of punishment that marked them, unenlightened as they still were, calling their attention to the fact that they were seeking not correction motivated by love, but vengeance in hatred.[159] So, after He had taught them what it is to love one's neighbor as oneself and had also infused into them the Holy Spirit whom He at the end of ten days after His ascension sent from above, as He had promised,[160] there were not wanting cases of vindictive punishment, though they were now far rarer than they had been under the Old Testament; for there, in the majority of cases, men were kept down by servile fear, while here they were brought up as free people by love. An instance of such a case of vindictive punishment was Ananias and his wife, who, as we read in the Acts of the Apostles, fell dead at the words of the Apostle Peter and were not brought back to life, but buried.[161]

65. But if heretics who are opposed to the Old Testament will deny this book authority,[162] let them cast eyes on the

Apostle Paul, whom they read with us, speaking about a certain sinner whom he delivered over *to Satan for the destruction
of the flesh that the soul may be saved.*[163] If they will not
here understand death—for perhaps it is uncertain—they will
have to admit that punishment of some kind was inflicted by
the Apostle through the instrumentality of Satan; and that
in this he was motivated not by hatred but love, is clear from
the addition *that the soul may be saved.* Or let them note
what we are saying, in those books to which they attach great
authority, where it is written that the Apostle Thomas cursed
a man who had buffeted him, calling down the punishment
of a horrible death; but his soul was prayed for, that it might
be spared in the world to come. The man was killed by a
lion, and a dog brought his hand severed from the rest of his
body to the table where the Apostle was dining.[164] We are
free to give no credence to this piece of writing, for it is not in
the Catholic canon; but they both, read it and honor it as
being most uncorrupted and most truthful, they who rave
most bitterly with a blindness that defies description, against
the corporal punishments which are in the Old Testament,
totally ignorant of the spirit and the temporal economy [165] in
which these punishments were inflicted.

66. Wherefore, in this category of indignities which are
expiated by punishment, this is the Christian rule of conduct:
when an indignity has been received, the mind is not to be
excited into hatred, but, taking compassion on the weakness
shown, it is to show itself ready to suffer more; nor is it to
neglect correction, to which end it may employ either advice
or authority or force.

Another is the category of indignities which can be completely adjusted, of which there are two classes: the one has
to do with money; the other, with an effort put forth. And

here, regarding the first, the example of the coat and garment was posited; in the second, that of being obliged to go one or two miles. For a garment can be given back; and he whom you assist by the effort you put forth can, if need be, help you.

Unless, perchance, we should distinguish as follows: that in the first case, regarding the cheek that was struck, there is reference to everything done in such a manner by wicked persons that adjustment is impossible save by punishment; second, what was posited about the garment may signify everything which can be adjusted without punishment; and so, perhaps, there was added *if a man will contend with thee in judgment,* because what is taken away on the basis of a sentence in court is not regarded as taken by force such as demands a penalty. But a third case may be construed from a joining of the two, so that an adjustment without and with punishment is possible: for instance, when a person without going to court makes a violent demand for service which is not due, as he does who wickedly constrains another and without benefit of law forces him against his will to assist him, he can both pay the penalty of his baseness and make a return for the service given, if he who has endured the wrong should ask it.

In all these types of indignities, therefore, the Lord teaches that the spirit of a Christian ought to be most patient and most compassionate and ever ready to endure more.

67. But because it means little not to harm unless also you bestow what benefit you can, He consequently goes on to say: *Give to everyone that asketh of thee and from him that would borrow of thee turn not away. To everyone that asketh,* He says; not " everything to one that asketh ": you are to give what you can give with propriety and justice. For,

what if he asks for money to enable him to oppress an innocent person? What, in fine, if he should make a lewd request? But, not to specify the many possibilities, for they are
innumerable, surely that is to be given which brings harm
neither to yourself nor to the other party so far as such
knowledge or assumption is humanly possible. And if you
have a good reason for refusing a request, you must indicate
that reason, that you do not send him away empty-handed.
In this way you will give to everybody who asks of you,
though not always will you give what he asks for. And sometimes you will give him something better, when you put on
the right course one who is asking for something that is not
right.

68. Then, as to what He says, *From him that would borrow of thee turn not away*, is to be referred to the disposition;
for *God loveth a cheerful giver*.[166] Whoever receives a thing
is a borrower even if he is not going to pay back. For, since
God gives back to the merciful more than they give, everyone
who confers a kindness lends at interest. Or if you will not
grant that the borrower should be taken as other than one
who receives with the intention of making due return, you
must understand that the Lord included both kinds of giving;
for either we bestow as a gift what we give in kindness, or
we lend to one who is willing to pay us back.

And for the most part men who are ready to give outright
with God's reward in mind become reluctant to give what is
asked of them as a loan, on the supposition that God will not
reward them because a thing loaned is given back. Rightly,
therefore, divine teaching encourages us in this way of conferring a favor, saying, *and from him that would borrow of
thee turn not away*; that is, do not deny your sympathy to one
who asks of you because you think your money will be un-

productive and God will not repay you because the borrower will; whereas if you do that out of respect for God's precept, it cannot be unproductive with Him who gives these commands.

CHAPTER 21

Love of enemies.

69. Then He goes on and says: *You have heard that it hath been said, " Thou shalt love thy neighbor and hate thy enemy." But I say to you, love your enemies, do good to them that hate you, and pray for them that persecute you;* [167] *that you may be the children of your Father who is in heaven, who commandeth His sun to rise upon the good and bad and raineth upon the just and the unjust. For if you love them that love you, what reward shall you have? Do not even the publicans this? And if you salute your brethren only, what do you more? Do not also the heathens this same thing? Be you therefore perfect as also your heavenly Father is perfect* (43-48). Yes, without this love wherewith we are commanded to love even our enemies and persecutors, who can do full justice to what has just been said? But the perfection of mercy that especially serves a soul in distress cannot go beyond love of an enemy; and, therefore, the conclusion: *Be you therefore perfect as also your heavenly Father is perfect.* Yet this is to be taken that God is perfect as God and the soul perfect as a soul.

70. That the righteousness of the Pharisees which was formed on the Old Law represents an advance of a sort is seen from the fact that there are many men who hate even

those who actually love them; for instance, spendthrift sons who hate their parents for curbing their spending. He, then, does make some advance who loves his fellow man though he still hates his enemy. Following the command of Him who came to fulfill the Law,[168] not to destroy it, a person will perfect his good will and kindness by the time he has brought it to love of enemy. For his initial step forward, although it is something, is still so small that it can characterize the publicans as well. And as to what is said in the Law, *thou shalt hate thy enemy*, is not to be taken as a command to the virtuous, but as a concession to the weak in virtue.[169]

71. Here arises a problem that surely cannot be ignored: Many passages in Scripture, if read superficially and without much reflection, seem to go counter to this precept of the Lord wherein He admonishes us to love our enemies, do good to them that hate us, and pray for those who persecute us; for in the Prophets we find many imprecations against enemies which are held to be curses, as is this: *Let their table become as a snare*,[170] and other things which are said there; and this one: *May his children be fatherless and his wife a widow*,[171] and others earlier and later in the same Psalm directed by the Prophet against the person of Judas. Many other texts are found everywhere in Scripture which may appear to be counter both to this precept of the Lord and to the Apostle's where he says, *Bless, and curse not* [172]— though in the case of the Lord it is written that He cursed the cities which had not received His word,[173] and the Apostle referred to said of someone: *The Lord will reward him according to his works*.[174]

72. But these difficulties are easily solved. For the Prophet

by his imprecation predicted what was going to happen—and this was not a wishful prayer but his spirit in the act of foreseeing. So also the Lord, so also the Apostle; though in the words of these, too, is found not what they wished but what they predicted. When, for example, the Lord said, *Woe to thee, Capharnaum,*[175] He states no more than that some evil is about to happen to her because of her unbelief.[176] What was impending the Lord did not malevolently wish, but saw by reason of His divinity. And the Apostle did not say: "May God reward—" but *God will reward him according to his works,* which is the expression of one making a prediction, not of one calling down a curse. So also with regard to the hypocrisy of the Jews which has already been mentioned and the destruction of which he saw was imminent, he said: *God shall strike thee, thou whited wall.*[177]

The Prophets especially are wont to predict the future in the manner of one pronouncing a curse, just as they have often spoken of the future in terms of the past; as, for instance, in that passage: *Why have the Gentiles raged and the people devised vain things?*[178] He did not say: "Why *will* the Gentiles rage and why *will* the people devise vain things?"[179] even though he was not mentioning these things as if they had already taken place, but was foreseeing them as yet to come. Such is also the case in the passage: *They parted my garments amongst them and upon my vesture they cast lots.*[180] Here again he did not say: "They will part my garments amongst them and upon my vesture they will cast lots." And yet no one finds fault with these words but him who does not realize that such variation of expression does not at all change the truth of things and adds much to the impressions made on our souls.

CHAPTER 22

The sin against the Holy Spirit. Are we to pray
for—or even against—those who commit it?

73. But a statement of the Apostle John makes our present problem more acute: *If a man knoweth his brother to sin a sin which is not to death, he shall ask; and the Lord shall give life to him who sinneth not unto death. But there is a sin unto death: for that I say not that any man ask.*[181] He clearly shows that there are some brethren for whom we are not commanded to pray, whereas the Lord commands us to pray even for our persecutors. Nor can we solve this difficulty unless we admit that there are some sins among the brethren that are more heinous than the persecution of enemies. That "brethren" means "Christians" can be proved by many examples from the divine Scriptures. But the most striking is the one put by the Apostle in these words: *For the unbelieving husband is sanctified by the wife and the unbelieving woman is sanctified by the brother.*[182] For he did not add "our"; he took that for granted, for by the term "brother" he meant to be understood a Christian who had a non-Christian wife. And therefore a little further on he says: *But if the unbeliever depart, let him depart. A brother or sister is not under servitude in such cases.*[183]

I think, therefore, that the sin of a brother is unto death when there is opposition to the brotherhood by one who has come to the knowledge of God through the grace of Our Lord Jesus Christ and against that grace, by which he was reconciled to God, he is stirred by the prods of contention.[184] The sin that is not unto death is the case of one who does not cut off the love for his brother, but through some infirmity of soul fails to perform the brotherly offices to which he is obligated. Wherefore also the Lord on the Cross said: *Father, forgive them; for they know not what they do.*[185] For they had not yet been made sharers in the grace of the Holy Spirit and so had not entered the society of the holy brotherhood. And the blessed Stephen, in the Acts of the Apostles,[186] prays for those who stone him; for they had not yet come to believe in Christ, and so were not contending against a grace that they shared with others. For this reason, too, I believe the Apostle Paul does not pray for Alexander; because he was already a brother and had sinned unto death, that is, attacked the brotherhood through envy. For those, however, who had not broken off their love, but had succumbed to fear, he prays that they may be pardoned. For this is what he says: *Alexander the coppersmith hath done me much evil; the Lord will reward him according to his works; whom do thou also avoid, for he hath greatly withstood our words.* He further adds for whom he does pray, saying thus: *At my first answer no man stood with me but all forsook me. May it not be laid to their charge!*[187]

74. It is this difference in their sins which distinguishes Judas the betrayer from Peter the denier. Not that pardon must not be extended to one who repents, for then we should be opposing the Lord's direction requiring that pardon must always be extended when brother asks brother for pardon;[188] but the infamy of that sin is so great that he cannot submit to the humiliation of praying even though his guilty conscience should force him to make open acknowledgment of his sin. For, though Judas had said: *I have sinned because I have betrayed innocent blood,*[189] it was easier for him to run and hang himself in despair than humbly to ask for forgiveness.

And therefore much depends on the quality of repentance to merit God's pardon. For many there are who are quick enough to say that they have sinned and who are so angry with themselves that they vehemently wish they had not sinned; yet they do not give up their pride so as to have an humble and contrite heart and to ask forgiveness; and this disposition of mind, so we must conclude, they have from a sense of already being condemned because of the greatness of their sin.

75. And this is perhaps the sin against the Holy Spirit, namely through malice and envy to antagonize brotherly love after receiving the grace of the Holy Spirit, which sin the Lord says is pardoned neither here nor in the world to come.[190] Hence one may ask whether the Jews sinned against the Holy Spirit when they said that the Lord was casting out devils by Beelzebub, prince of devils;[191] whether we are to take the remark as addressed to the Lord Himself, because in another place He says of Himself: *For if they have called the Master of the house Beelzebub, how much more them of His household?*[192] Or, since they had spoken out of great envy and without appreciation of the benefits being conferred, though as yet they had not become Christians, yet because of the very intensity of their envy can they be thought to have sinned against the Holy Spirit? No; this is not evident in the words of the Lord. For, although in the same context He said: *For whosoever shall speak an evil word against the Son of man, it shall be forgiven him; but he that shall speak against the Holy Ghost, it shall not be forgiven him, neither in this world nor in the world to come,*[193] yet it is possible to take this as the intent of His warning: to have them come to His grace and after receiving it not to sin as they just now sinned. For now they spoke an evil word against the Son of

man, and that can be pardoned them if they will be converted and believe in Him and receive the Holy Spirit. If they do receive the Spirit and then deliberately envy the brotherhood and assail the grace they have received, they cannot be forgiven, neither in this life nor in the next. For if He regarded them as so far gone as to have no last hope of pardon, He would not judge that they should still be warned, which He did by saying: *Either make the tree good and its fruits good, or make the tree evil and its fruits evil.*[194]

76. Therefore the precept to love our enemies, to do good to those who hate us, to pray for those who persecute us may thus be interpreted as to imply that for some sins even of the brethren we are not commanded to pray. Otherwise, because we are so ill-qualified to interpret it, divine Scripture would appear self-contradictory, a thing that cannot be. But whether, as for certain ones prayer is not to be offered, so, too, we are to pray against some—this has not yet become sufficiently clear. For it is said in general, *Bless, and curse not*; and again: *to no man rendering evil for evil.*[195] When you do not pray for a person, you do not therefore pray against him. For you can see his punishment as a certainty and his salvation utterly despaired of; and not because you hate him, do you not pray for him; but because you feel you can avail him nothing and you do not want your prayer rejected by a most just Judge.

But what stand do we take regarding those against whom we are told the saints prayed—not for their conversion, for that would be praying for them, but for that damnation from which there is no return; not as was done against the Lord's betrayer by the Prophet, for, as was said, that was a prediction of future events, not a wish for punishment; nor as by the Apostle against Alexander, regarding which also I have already said enough; but as we read in the Apocalypse of John,[196] of the martyrs praying that they might be avenged, while that first martyr prayed for the pardon of those who were stoning him?

77. But this must not disturb us. For who would be bold enough to say whether, when those white-robed saints prayed for their vindication, they prayed against those men or against the kingdom of sin? This is the actual vindication of the martyrs—a vindication that bears with it the fullness of justice and mercy—that the kingdom of sin be overthrown during whose existence they suffered such grievous things.[197] The Apostle's best is given to its overthrow when he says, *Let not sin, therefore, reign in your mortal body.*[198] The kingdom of sin is utterly destroyed partly through the correction of men bringing about the subjection of the flesh to the spirit, partly by the damnation of those who persist in sin, so that justice puts them in their place and they cannot cause trouble to the just who reign with Christ. Look at the Apostle Paul. Does he not seem to you to be vindicating in himself the martyr Stephen when he says: *I do not so fight as one beating the air; but I chastise my body and bring it into subjection?* [199] In this way indeed was he putting down in himself and keeping down and reforming the way of life by which he had persecuted Stephen and the other Christians. Who, therefore, can prove that the holy martyrs were not asking the Lord for a like vindication of themselves, when they could also legitimately ask towards their own vindication the end of this world wherein they had borne such sufferings? And, praying for this, they both pray for their enemies who can be restored and on the other hand do not pray against those who choose to forego restoration; because God in punishing them is not a malevolent torturer but a most just

maintainer of order. Without hesitancy, therefore, let us love our enemies, let us do good to those who hate us, and let us pray for those who persecute us.

CHAPTER 23

We are children of God through adoption. God's spiritual sun and rain. Recapitulation.

78. Then, regarding what follows: *that you may be the children of your Father who is in heaven,* this is to be understood according to that rule of conduct which also prompted John to say: *He gave them power to be made sons of God.*[200] There is but one Son by nature, who knows nothing at all of sin; but we are made sons, by an opportunity that we receive, in so far as we carry out what He prescribes. Hence the Apostle in his teaching calls this an adoption, whereby we are called to an eternal inheritance to become coheirs with Christ.[201] We, therefore, become sons of God by a spiritual rebirth and are adopted into the kingdom of God not as though we were strangers, but as made and created by Him. Thus there is the one kindness, His having created us by His almighty power when before we were nothing; and the other, whereby He adopted us that as sons we might enjoy with Him eternal life to the measure of our participation. Hence He did not say: " Do these things *because* you are children "; but: " Do these things *in order that* you may be children."

79. And when God calls us to this through the Only-begotten Himself, He calls us to His own likeness. For, as He goes on to say: He *maketh His sun to rise upon the good and bad and raineth upon the just and the unjust.* You may

interpret " His sun " to be not that one which is visible to the human eye, but that wisdom about which it is said: *for she is the brightness of eternal life,*[202] and of which, again, it is said: *the Sun of justice is risen unto me,* and again: *But unto you that fear the name of the Lord the Sun of justice shall arise* [203]—so that then you would also take " the rain " to be the watering of the teaching of truth, because it has appeared to the good and the bad, and the good message of Christ has been given to the good and the bad. Or you may prefer to interpret it as the sun made conspicuous to the physical eyes not only of men but also of beasts, and the rain as that by which products are brought forth that have been given for the restoration of the body—a more probable interpretation, I think: so that the spiritual sun rises only upon the good and holy, for this is the very thing the wicked complain of in that book which is entitled the Wisdom of Solomon, *The sun hath not risen upon us;* [204] and the spiritual rain refreshes none but the good, for the wicked are signified by the vine about which it is said, *I will command my clouds not to rain upon it.*[205] But whether you accept the one or the other, if we wish to be sons of God, this is realized through the great goodness of God which we are commanded to imitate. How much relief in this life this visible light and material rain afford, who is so ungrateful as not to sense this? And this relief we see conferred in this life on the just and on sinners alike. He did not merely say: *who maketh the sun to rise upon the good and bad;* but He added the word " His," that is, which He Himself made and set up and for the making of which He took something from nothing, as is written in Genesis [206] of all the luminaries; and He can properly say that all the things created by Him out of nothing are His own. Thus we are reminded of how generously we must, according to His precept, extend to our enemies the things which we have not created but only received from His munificence.

80. But who can be ready to put up with indignities from the weak to the extent that it is beneficial to their salvation; and prefer to suffer more of another's unfair treatment than to pay him back for what he has already suffered; to give to everyone that asks something from him whether that something is a thing he possesses and can lawfully give or consists of the giving of good advice and sympathy; nor to turn away from one who wants to borrow; to love enemies, do good to those who hate him, and pray for those who persecute him—who can do these things but one who is utterly and perfectly merciful? And by this counsel alone is misery kept away, He helping who says: *I desire mercy rather than sacrifice.*[207] Therefore, *Blessed are the merciful, for they shall obtain mercy.*[208]

But now I think it agreeable that at this point the reader, tired by the length of this treatise, should breathe a little and freshen his interest for considering what is reserved for another book.

BOOK TWO

The Latter Part of the Lord's Sermon on the Mount,
Contained in the Sixth and Seventh
Chapters of Matthew

CHAPTER 1

*Right living consists in striving to please God,
not man.*

1. The subject of mercy, the treatment of which brought
us to the close of the first book, is followed by that of the
cleansing of the heart, with which the present one begins.
The cleansing of the heart is, as it were, a cleansing of the
eye by which God is seen; and to keep it clear [1] requires care
commensurate with the worth of the object this eye sees.
Once we have cleansed this eye in good part, it is difficult to
prevent particles of dirt from finding their way in unnoticed—
from the things that usually go with our good actions, as,
for instance, human praise. If it is true that not to live well
leads to ruin; but to live well and yet not wish to be praised—
what is this but to be an enemy of human ways, which surely
are the more to be pitied the less the good lives of men meet
with approval? Therefore, if the people with whom you live
do not praise you for your right living, they are at fault; but
if they do praise you, you are in danger—unless you are so
single-hearted and pure that what you do as you should you do

not do because of men's praise; and that you give credit to those who praise what is right because they delight in good, rather than to yourself, because you would live uprightly even if no one praised you; and that you realize that praise accorded you redounds to the benefit of those who praise you if they honor not you for your good life, but God, whose most holy temple everyone is who leads a good life; so that what David said is fulfilled: *In the Lord shall my soul be praised; let the meek hear and rejoice.*[a]

Therefore it belongs to the clean eye not to look for the praise of men in any right conduct nor to associate one's good conduct with any idea of praise, that is, doing the right thing just to please men. For you will be disposed also to simulate good, if your only consideration is man's praise, because he, unable to see the heart, may praise even what is false. And those who do this, that is, who simulate goodness, have duplicity in their hearts. The heart of simplicity, that is, the clean heart, belongs only to him who lives beyond human praise and in his right living looks only to Him and strives to please only Him who alone reads the conscience. And whatever proceeds from the purity of such a conscience is praise-deserving in proportion to its lack of desire for human praise.

2. *Take heed* therefore, He says, *that you do not your justice before men, to be seen by them* (6. 1): that is, guard against living an upright life from this motive and making your good lie in this, that men may see you. *Otherwise you shall not have a reward of your Father who is in heaven* (1): not if you are seen by men; but if you live uprightly for this reason, that you be seen by men. But what is to become of what was said in the beginning of this sermon: *You are the light of the world. A city seated on a mountain cannot be hid.*

Neither do men light a candle and put it under a bushel, but upon a candlestick, that it may shine to all that are in the house. So let your light shine before men that they may see your good works? But He did not stop there; He added: *and glorify your Father who is in heaven* (5. 14-16). But here, because He is reprehending the case of our good actions stopping there, that is, if we act uprightly for this reason, that we be seen only by men, after He had said: *Take heed that you do not your justice before men, to be seen by them,* He added nothing. From this it is evident that He had not forbidden that we do what is right before men, but our doing right before men merely to be seen by them, that is, to have this as our objective and therein place the motivation of what we propose to do.

3. The Apostle also says: *If I yet pleased men, I should not be the servant of Christ;*[3] whereas in another place he says: *Please all men in all things, as I also in all things please all men.*[4] People who do not understand this find in it a contradiction. What he actually said was that he did not please men, because he was doing right not simply to please men, but God, to whose love he wished to turn the hearts of men by the very thing in which he was pleasing men. Therefore he was right in saying that he pleased not men, because he was bent solely on this, to please God. And he was right in laying down the precept to please all men, not that this should be sought as the reward of good conduct, but because that person could not please God who would not propose himself as exemplar to those whom he wished to save; for it is utterly impossible for anyone to imitate another who does not please him. As, therefore, he would not be speaking foolishly who would say: " In this my effort of looking for a ship, I am not seeking a ship but my fatherland," so also the

Apostle might appositely say: "In this my effort of pleasing men, I please not men but God; because I have no desire to please men, but I do have this in mind, that those I wish to save would imitate me." As he says in reference to the contributions made for the saints: *Not that I seek the gift, but I seek the fruit;*[5] that is, "As to what I am seeking as your gift, it is not the gift I am seeking but the profit to come therefrom for you." For by such a token it could become apparent what progress they had made towards God, when they should offer willingly what was asked of them, not prompted by the joy over their offerings, but by the bond of charity uniting them.

4. But yet, when He also goes on to say: *Otherwise you shall not have a reward of your Father who is in heaven,* He points out only this: that we must be on our guard not to seek human praise as the reward of our good deeds, that is, not to think that we are made blessed thereby.

CHAPTER 2

Hypocrisy. In performing good works we must be single-hearted.

5. *Therefore,* He said, *when thou dost an almsdeed, sound not a trumpet before thee, as the hypocrites do in the synagogues and in the streets, that they may be glorified by men* (2). Do not, He said, desire to become known, as the hypocrites do. Now, it is manifest that hypocrites do not carry in their heart what they flash before the eyes of men. Hypocrites are pretenders, like mouthpieces of other persons, as in the plays of the theatre. For one who in tragedy takes the

part of Agamemnon, for example, or of any other person involved in the story or myth being enacted, is not really the person himself, but impersonates him and is called a *hypocrita*.⁶ So, too, in the Church or in any phase of human life, whoever wishes to seem what he actually is not is a hypocrite. He pretends to be a right-doing person, but is not such in practice. The whole purpose of his behavior is to win the praise of men. This mere pretenders can win, too, deceiving those to whom they seem good and by whom they are consequently praised. But from God, the Observer of hearts,⁷ they receive no reward but punishment for their deceit; and from men, He says, *they have received their reward* (2); and most justly will it be said to them: *Depart from me, ye workers of deceit*; ⁸ you bore my name, but you did not do my works. Those, therefore, *have received their reward* who give alms with no other intent than to receive acclaim from men; not, if they receive acclaim from men, but if they act with the intention of receiving acclaim, as has been set forth above. Praise of men should not be sought by a person who does the right thing, that they may benefit who can also imitate what they praise; not, that he should think they are in any way benefitting him whom they praise.

6. *But when thou dost alms, let not thy left hand know what thy right hand doth* (3). Should you interpret the "left hand" as meaning unbelievers, no fault will be seen in wishing to please believers, whereas we are nonetheless strictly forbidden to place the fruit and purpose of our good work in the praise of any man whatever. But as to having people imitate you, who see with satisfaction your good works, we must give this opportunity not only to believers, but also to unbelievers, that in praising our good deeds they may honor God and come to salvation. If, however, you hold the

"left hand" to mean an enemy, so that your enemy is not to know when you give an alms, why did the Lord Himself in compassion cure people in the very presence of His enemies, the Jews? Further, why did the Apostle Peter bring on himself and other disciples of Christ the wrath of his enemies by curing a lame man whom he pitied at the Beautiful Gate? Besides, if an enemy is not to know when we give an alms, how are we to deal with that same enemy so as to fulfill the precept: *If thy enemy be hungry, give him to eat; if he thirst, give him to drink?* [10]

7. There is always a third opinion, so absurd and ridiculous that I would not mention it if I did not know from my own experience that not a few are attracted by the error: it is held by people with carnal minds who say that the term "left hand" stands for "wife"; that since women in managing the home generally are rather tenacious of money, they are kept in the dark when their husbands in pity spend something upon the needy, for fear of domestic quarrels. So we are to think that only husbands are Christians and that this precept has not been given to women also! From what left hand, then, is a wife enjoined to conceal her work of mercy? Is the husband in turn to be the wife's left hand? How utterly ridiculous! Or let some one think that they are left hands to each other: then, if anything of the family purse is expended by the one party in a manner contrary to the wish of the other, such a marriage will not be a Christian one. But it is inescapable that when either of them decides to give an alms in accordance with God's command and meets with opposition from the other, then the latter is an enemy of the command of God and is therefore to be classed among unbelievers; and as to such, there is the precept that by their good companionship and behavior the believing husband

should win his wife over or the believing wife her husband.[11] Wherefore, they should not conceal from each other their good deeds by which they are to be mutually attracted so that one may be able to draw the other into the communion of the Christian faith. Nor are thefts to be committed in order to make oneself acceptable to God. And if anything is to be concealed as long as the weakness of the other party cannot calmly put up with what it is right and permitted to do, still that the wife is not here signified by the " left hand," is quite apparent from a consideration of the entire context; and from this it will also be found what He calls the " left hand."

8. *Take heed*, He said, *that you do not your justice before men, to be seen by them; otherwise you shall not have a reward of your Father who is in heaven.* Here He has mentioned justice in general, then He goes on to particularize. For some part of justice is the work done by giving alms; so He makes the connection and says: *Therefore, when thou dost an almsdeed, sound not a trumpet before thee, as the hypocrites do in the synagogues and in the streets, that they may be glorified by men.* Here there is a reference to what He said before: *Take heed that you do not your justice before men, to be seen by them*; and what follows: *Amen, I say to you, they have received their reward*, refers to what He stated above: *otherwise you shall not have a reward of your Father who is in heaven.* Then follows: *But when thou dost an almsdeed.* When He says " But when thou " what else is He saying but " not as they "? What, then, does He bid us do? *But when thou dost alms, let not thy left hand know what thy right hand doth.* Those others act in such a way that their left hand knows what their right hand is doing. What, therefore, was blamed in them, this you are forbidden to do. In them it was blamed that they act to gain the ap-

plause of men. For this reason there seems no more logical explanation than that the "left hand" stands for just this delight in praise. The "right hand" signifies the determination to carry out the divine precepts. When, therefore, to the consciousness of giving alms is associated the craving for human praise, the left hand is made conscious of the work of the right hand. Hence, *Let not the left hand know what the right hand doth*—that is, let no desire for human praise be in your thoughts when in the giving of alms you are trying to carry out what God prescribed.

9. *That thy alms may be in secret* (4). What is the meaning of "in secret" but simply "in a good conscience," which conscience it is impossible to show to human eyes or to reveal in words, and this the more as there are many persons given to lying in many things? Wherefore, if the right hand acts in secret within the soul, then to the left hand belongs all that is external, all the visible and temporal. Let your alms, therefore, be in your own inner self, where many a one gives alms through his good will even if he has no money or anything else to give to the needy. But many give outwardly and not from within—those who, either seeking recognition or motivated by some temporal object, want to appear merciful. In their case only the left hand is to be considered as working. Again, there are others holding, as it were, a middle course: they actually direct their intention towards God when they give an alms, yet at the same time there creeps into this excellent intention not a little craving for praise or for a perishable and transitory object of some sort or other. But Our Lord's emphasis in forbidding that the left hand alone work in us is all the stronger since He forbids even that the left become involved in what the right hand does: that is to say, that we should not only beware of giving

an alms motivated solely by desire for temporal things; but that in this work we are also not to regard God in such a manner as to involve a blending or uniting with a grasping after external interests. For here there is question of cleansing the heart, which, unless it is a single heart, will not be clean. And how can it be a single heart if it serves two masters and does not keep its sight clear by giving eternal things its only attention, but bedims it by the love of mortal and transitory things as well? Therefore *let thy alms be in secret; and thy Father who sees in secret will repay thee* (4). This is the truth in most precise terms. For if you look for a reward from the one who alone can read the conscience, that conscience should suffice you in meriting a reward.

Many Latin versions of this text read: *And thy Father who sees in secret will reward thee openly*; but because we failed to find the word " openly " in the Greek texts which are earlier, we did not think that any comment was called for.[12]

CHAPTER 3

Prayer.

10. *And when ye pray, you shall not be as the hypocrites that love to stand and pray in the synagogues and corners of the streets that they may be seen by men* (5). Here again it is not the being seen by men that is wrong, but doing these things in order that you may be seen by men. And it is superfluous to say the same thing over and over again, since there is just one rule we have to observe, from which we know that what we should fear and avoid is not that men know these things, but that our motive in doing them should be to seek

after the fruit that comes from pleasing men. The Lord Himself, too, has these very same words in mind when He adds similarly: *Amen I say to you, they have received their reward*, showing thereby that His prohibition is directed against seeking that kind of reward in which fools delight when they are praised by men.

11. *But when you pray, enter into your chambers* (6). What are these " chambers " but the hearts themselves which are also signified in the Psalm when it is said: *The things you say in your hearts, also be sorry for them upon your beds.*[13] *And, after having closed the doors,* He says, *pray to your Father in secret* (6). It is not enough to merely go into the chamber, leaving the door open to the importunate: in through the door plunge without shame the things that are outside and they make for the privacy of ourselves.[14] The things without, we have said, are all the transitory and visible things which through the open door, that is, our fleshly senses, noise in upon us while we pray with a whirl of idle fancies. Therefore the door must be closed—we must resist our carnal senses so that the prayer of our spirit may be directed to the Father; and this arises from the depths of our heart when we *pray to the Father in secret.*

And your Father, He says, *who seeth in secret will repay you* (6). And here a conclusion such as we have in these words was called for; for here He is not teaching us to pray, but how to pray;—nor above, that we should give alms, but in what spirit we are to give them. After all, He is setting down a rule for the cleansing of the heart; and the only thing that makes it clean is the undivided and single-minded striving after eternal life from pure love of wisdom alone.

12. *And when you are praying*, says He, *speak not much,*

as the heathens. For they think that in their much speaking they may be heard (7). As it is a mark of hypocrites to bring themselves to the attention of others when they pray, the fruit of which is to please men, so it is a mark of heathens, that is, Gentiles,[15] to think that in their saying much they are being heard. And in fact all profuseness in speaking [16] comes from the Gentiles, who devote their energies to exercising their tongue rather than to keeping their heart clean. And this kind of trivial exertion they make effort to transfer also to the influencing of God through prayer, supposing that the Judge, just like man, is brought over by words to decide for them. *Be not you, therefore, like to them,* says the only true Teacher,[17] *for your Father knoweth what is needful for you, before you ask of Him* (8). For if many words are resorted to in order to instruct and teach an ignorant person, what need is there of them in the presence of the Knower of all things, to whom all things speak by the very fact that they exist and their existence acknowledges that He made them? What need is there of them when, too, the things that lie in the future do not escape His knowledge and wisdom in which both the things that are past and those that will yet come to pass are all present and in no stage of passing?

13.   But since He Himself is about to speak words, though they be few, by which He will teach us to pray, it can be asked: What need even of those few words to Him who knows all things before they happen and knows, as was said, what we need before we ask Him? Here, first of all, the answer is that it is not words we should use in dealing with God to obtain what we want; but it is the things we carry in our mind and the direction of our thoughts, with pure love and single affection. The Lord made use of words to teach

us those very things that by committing them to memory we may remember them at the time of prayer.

14. But again it may be asked: Ignoring the question whether we need to pray by words or things—what need for that prayer at all if God already knows what we need? None, save that the very effort we make in praying calms the heart, makes it clean, and renders it more capable of receiving the divine gifts which are poured upon us in a spiritual manner. For God does not hear us because He seeks the favor of our prayers, He who is always ready to give us His light, not that which strikes the eye, but that of the intellect and spirit. But we are not always prepared to receive, attracted as we are to other things and benighted by our desire for temporal things. Hence there takes place in prayer a turning of the heart to Him who is ever ready to give if we will but accept what He gives. And in this turning there is effected a cleansing of the inner eye, consisting in the exclusion of those things which filled our earth-bound desires so that the vision of a pure heart may be able to bear the pure light, radiating from God without any diminution or setting; and not only to bear it, but also to remain in it, not merely without discomfort but with the unspeakable joy whereby truly and unequivocally a blessed life is perfected.

CHAPTER 4

How to pray. The model prayer.

15. But now we must consider what He has ordered us to pray for through whom we are both taught what to pray for and obtain what we pray for. *Thus, therefore,* He said, *do*

you pray: Our Father, who art in heaven, hallowed be Thy name; thy kingdom come, thy will be done, on earth as it is in heaven. Give us this day our daily bread; and forgive us our debts as we also forgive our debtors; and bring us not into temptation, but deliver us from evil (9-13).[18] Noting that in every request we have to win the kindly disposition in him of whom we make request, and then state what we pray for: it is by a laudation of him to whom the prayer is addressed that benevolence is gained; and this is regularly put at the beginning of the prayer. Touching this, the Lord has ordered us to say nothing else than *Our Father, who art in heaven.* A great deal has been said in praise of God in a variety of ways and in many places in Holy Scripture which anyone can reflect on when he reads them; but nowhere is found a command given the people of Isreal to say *Our Father,* or to pray to God as a *father;* but it was as *Master* that they knew Him, they being slaves, that is, still living according to the flesh. I say this, however, of the time when they received the commandments of the Law which they were told to observe. The Prophets, of course, often pointed out that this same Lord of ours might also have been their Father if they had not gone astray from His commandments; as, for instance, in this statement: *I have brought up children and exalted them, but they have despised me;* [19] and in this: *I have said: You are gods, and all of you the sons of the Most High;* [20] and again: *If I be a master, where is my fear? If I be a Father, where is my honor?* [21] and there are numerous other instances in which the Jews are arraigned for refusing by their sins to be God's children. Exceptions are those things that were said in prophecy about the future Christian people, that they would have God as a Father, according to that celebrated Gospel text: *He gave them power to be made sons of*

God; [22] and the Apostle Paul says: *As long as the heir is a child, he differeth nothing from a servant*; [23] and he mentions that we have received *the spirit of adoption whereby we cry Abba, Father.*[24]

16. And because the fact that we are called to an eternal inheritance to be coheirs with Christ and come into the adoption of sons [25] is not owing to any merit of ours, but to the grace of God, we therefore put that same grace at the beginning of our prayer, saying, *Our Father*. And by this term both love is stimulated—for what ought to be dearer to children than their father?—and a suppliant spirit, too, when men say to God: *Our Father*; and almost a taking for granted that we are going to obtain what we are about to ask for, because before we make any request we have already received so great a gift as to be permitted to say to God, *Our Father*. Indeed, what would He not give His children asking Him, when He has already given them this great thing in advance, that they should be His children! Lastly, what responsibility rests upon the soul of taking care that he who says *Our Father* be not unworthy of such a Father! If a plebeian should receive express permission from a senator of more advanced age to call him father, he would quite certainly become excited and would hardly dare do so, aware of his lowly origin and his lack of means and his own ordinary person. How much greater, then, should be our trepidation in calling God *Father* if we are so tainted and debased of character that God might much more justly keep these qualities from contact with Himself than the senator the poverty of some nondescript beggar! For, indeed, the senator is repulsing in the beggar the status to which he himself might come through the precariousness of human fortunes, whereas God never lapses into baseness of character. And thanks be to His compassion

who requires this of us that He should be our Father—a relationship that cannot be acquired at any price but only through His benevolence. Here there is also an admonition to the rich and to those who in the eyes of the world are well-born, that when they become Christians they are not to lord it over the poor and the lowly; because they are one in saying to God, *Our Father*, which they cannot say with true piety unless they recognize that they are their brothers.

CHAPTER 5

" Our Father, who art in Heaven ": God dwells
in His Saints as His temple; " hallowed
be Thy name ": the Gospel is being
preached everywhere.

17. Therefore let the new people called to an eternal inheritance use the language of the New Testament and say: *Our Father, who art in heaven*—that is, among the saints and the just. God is not tied down to space or place. The heavens, truly enough, are the most excellent physical bodies of the universe; just the same, bodies they are, and bodies can be only in space. But if God's place is believed to be in the heavens as the more elevated parts of the universe, then the birds count more than we, for their life is lived nearer to God. However, it is not written: " God is nigh to men on high " or " to the mountain dwellers "; but it is written, *The Lord is nigh unto them that are of a contrite heart;* [26] and that refers rather to humility. And just as the sinner has been called earth, when to him it was said: *Earth thou art and unto earth thou shalt return;* [27] so, on the other hand, the just

can be called heaven, for to the just it is said: *For the temple of God is holy, which you are.*[28] Wherefore, if God dwells in His temple and the saints are His temple, the words *who art in heaven* are rightly said to be the equivalent of "who art in the saints." And this equation is a most appropriate one, indicating as it does that there is as much difference spiritually between a sinner and a saint as there is materially between heaven and earth.

18. For the purpose of signifying this fact, when we stand at prayer we turn to the east [29] whence the sky rises; not as if God were dwelling there and, as it were, had deserted the rest of the universe—He who is present everywhere, not in the spacings of places but by the power of His majesty. Our purpose is to impress upon our soul to turn to a more excellent nature, that is, to God, seeing that the body itself which is earthly, is turned to a more excellent body, that is, to a heavenly body.[30] Further, it is proper and eminently beneficial to the stages of religion that the senses of all, both young and old, be sensitive to God. And therefore, regarding those who are as yet given to the visible realm of beauty and cannot conceive of anything immaterial, because they have only the choice of preferring the heavens to the earth, one can be the more satisfied with their outlook if they, still thinking of God in terms of matter, consider Him to be in the heavens rather than on earth. Thus, when they eventually come to learn that the worth of a soul surpasses even a heavenly body, they will seek Him in the soul rather than in a heavenly body. And once they learn all that separates the souls of sinners and the virtuous, as they did not dare when all their thoughts were earth-bound to assign Him to earth, but to the heavens, so afterwards with a better faith and understanding they will look for Him in the souls of the

virtuous rather than in the souls of sinners. Correctly, therefore, the words, *Our Father, who art in heaven,* are taken as being tantamount to saying " in the hearts of the virtuous as His holy temple." And thus at the same time, praying he will wish that He whom he invokes may dwell in him also; and when this is his striving, he will be practicing right living; and when this is done, God is invited to make the soul His home.

19. And now, having stated who He is who is prayed to and where He dwells, let us see what we are to pray for. The first of all the things which are to be asked for is this: *Hallowed be Thy name.* This petition is not so worded as if God's name were not already holy, but that men may regard it as holy, that is, that God may become so familiar to them that they will esteem nothing more holy and dread nothing more than to offend that name. And certainly, because it was said: *In Judea God is known; His name is great in Israel,*[31] this is not to be understood as if God were less in one place and more in another; but there His name is great where it is mentioned because of the greatness of His majesty. So, too, there His name is pronounced holy where it is mentioned with reverence and the fear of offending Him. And this is precisely what is now transpiring: the Gospel by being made known among all the different nations even in our own times commends the name of the one God through the operation of His Son.[31a]

CHAPTER 6

"Thy kingdom come": the Lord's reign in the hearts of the just after the judgment. "Thy will be done on earth as it is in heaven": man's present state and his future destiny predicate a multifold accomplishment of God's will.

20. Then follows: *Thy kingdom come.* As the Lord Himself teaches in the Gospel that then will be the Day of Judgment when the Gospel shall have been preached among all nations: [32] we have here a matter that concerns the sanctification of God's name. For here, too, the words "Thy kingdom come" do not imply that God is not reigning now. But it might be said that with "come" we should supply "upon the earth." As if God were not even now reigning on earth and has not been doing so ever since the world was created! "Come," then, must be taken to mean "may it be made manifest to men." Just as light that is present is absent to the blind or to those who shut their eyes, so the kingdom of God, though it never departs from the earth, yet is absent to those who know nothing about it. To none, however, will ignorance of God's kingdom be permitted when His Only-begotten will come from heaven, not merely so that He is recognizable by the intellect, but visibly as the Man of the Lord [33] to judge the living and the dead. After this judgment, that is, when the selection of the just and their separation from the unjust has been made, God will so dwell in the just that there will be no need for anyone to be taught by man but *they shall all,* as it is written, *be taught of God.* [34] Then will

the blessed life be made perfect in all respects in the saints for eternity, even as now the most holy and blessed angels in heaven with God alone to enlighten them are wise and blessed, because the Lord promised this also to His followers: *In the resurrection, He says, they shall be as the angels in heaven.*[35]

21. And therefore, after the petition wherein we say: *Thy kingdom come,* there follows: *Thy will be done on earth as it is in heaven.* This means: " As Thy will is in the angels who are in heaven so that in every respect they remain close to Thee and fully enjoy Thee with no error bedimming their wisdom, no misery frustrating their blessedness, so may it be accomplished in Thy saints who are on earth and have been made from the earth as respects their body and, though they are to be taken up to be transformed and to dwell in heaven,[36] are yet on earth." There is also a reflection of this in the hymn of the angels: *Glory to God in the highest and on earth peace to men of good will.*[37] Thus when our good will has gone before by following Him when He calls, the will of God is accomplished in us as it is in the heavenly angels. Thus no adversity stands in the way of our happiness; and this is peace. Again, *Thy will be done,* correctly interpreted, means " let obedience be given to Thy precepts "— *on earth as it is in heaven,* that is, " by men as it is by angels." For that the will of God is being done when His precepts are obeyed the Lord Himself affirms when He says: *My meat is to do the will of Him who sent me;* [38] and often: *I have not come to do my own will, but the will of Him that sent me;* [39] and when He said: *Behold my mother and behold my brethren; and whosoever shall do the will of God, he is my brother and mother and sister.*[40] And therefore, in those at least who do God's will is the will of God accom-

plished—not because they make God will but because they
do as He wills, that is, they act according to His will.

22. There is also the other acceptation: *Thy will be done
on earth as it is in heaven*, that is, as in the holy and just,
so also in sinners. This, moreover, can be taken in two ways:
either that we also pray for our enemies—for how else are
they to be reckoned against whose will it is that the Christian
and Catholic name is being spread?—and then to say *Thy will
be done on earth as it is in heaven* amounts to saying: " As
the just so also may the sinners do Thy will, in order that
they may be converted to Thee "; or, *Thy will be done on
earth as it is in heaven*, that is, so that to each may be given
his due; and this will take place at the Last Judgment when
the sheep will be separated from the goats [41]—the just receiving a due reward, the sinners, the damnation due them.

23. The other acceptation is not absurd either, nay, it is
in perfect accordance with our faith and hope, namely, to
take heaven and earth as signifying spirit and flesh. And,
noting that the Apostle says: *With the mind I serve the law
of God, but with the flesh, the law of sin*,[42] we see the will
of God done in the mind, that is, in the spirit; but when
death shall be swallowed up in victory and *this corruptible
put on incorruption*,[43] which will happen at the resurrection
of the body and by that change which is promised to the just
according to the preaching of the same Apostle,[44] then may
the will of God be done also on earth as it is in heaven—that
is, as the spirit does not resist God, following and doing His
will, so also may the body not resist the spirit or soul, which
is now harassed by the body's infirmities and is prone to fall
in with the body's habits. And this will be of the essence of
supreme peace in the life eternal, that not only to wish the

good will attend us but also to effect it; *for now to will is present with me*, he says, *but to accomplish that which is good I find not.*[45] The reason is simply, that not yet on earth as in heaven, that is, not yet in the flesh as in the spirit, is the will of God done. For, it is true, even in our wretchedness God's will is being done, when we suffer in the flesh those things which are our due by the law of mortality, and this our nature has merited by sinning. But this we must pray for, that the will of God be done as in heaven so also on earth; in other words, that as in the heart *we are delighted with the law of God according to the inner man,*[46] so also a change in the body having been effected, nothing in us may, because of earthly griefs or pleasures, stand in the way of this our delight.

24. Nor does this clash with truth, that we interpret *Thy will be done on earth as it is in heaven* to mean " as in our Lord Jesus Christ Himself so also in the Church "; as in the Husband who fulfilled the Father's will, so also in the Woman espoused to Him.[47] Heaven and earth, it is plain, are appropriately thought of as husband and wife, for the earth is fruitful from the heaven giving it fecundity.[48]

CHAPTER 7

*" Give us this day our daily bread ": daily susten-
ance of the body, daily Holy Commun-
ion, daily sustenance of the spirit.*

25. The fourth petition is: *Give us this day our daily bread.* " Daily bread " [49] is said either of all that is necessary to sustain this life, concerning which He said by way of in-

struction: *Do not think of the morrow,*[50] so that for this reason there was added " give us *this day* "; or it was said of the Sacrament of Christ's Body which we receive daily; [51] or it is said of spiritual food, concerning which the same Lord Himself says: *Labor for the food which perisheth not;* [52] and again: *I am the bread of life which came down from heaven.*[53] But which of these three possibilities is the more probable, is a matter for earnest study. A person may wonder, for example, why we should pray to obtain those things which are necessary for life, such as food and clothing, when the Lord Himself says: *Be not solicitous what you shall eat or what you shall put on.*[54] Can anyone not be solicitous about the thing to obtain which he is praying, considering that prayer must be performed with such firm purpose of the mind that all which was said about closing the chambers applies here; so, too, His statement: *Seek ye first the kingdom of God and His justice, and all these things shall be added unto you?* [55] He did not at all say: " Seek first the kingdom of God, and then seek these things "; but *all these things,* He said, *shall be added unto you,* that is to say, though you are not seeking them. However, as to finding a justification for saying that a person is not seeking what he is not earnestly asking God for, I do not know whether this is possible.

26. Concerning the Sacrament of the Body of the Lord, that they may not raise a question who—the majority of them in the Orient—do not communicate of the Lord's Supper daily, though this Bread was called " daily bread "; [56] to keep them, therefore, from raising their voice or coming out in defense of their opinion even by church authority that they have this practice with no scandal being involved and are not forbidden this by those who preside over the churches and are

not condemned for this their non-observance—this merely goes to show that in those parts this Bread is not understood as " daily bread "; otherwise they would be subject to the charge of a grievous sin for not receiving daily. However, as has been said, not to discuss at all—one way or the other— the practice referred to: surely, this ought to occur to those who ponder on this, that we have received a rule of prayer from the Lord and that it must not be transgressed either by adding or omitting anything. This being the case, who is there who would venture to say that we ought to pray the Lord's Prayer only once, or at least that, granted we pray it a second or third time but only up to that hour when we receive the Body of the Lord, afterwards we are not to repeat the prayer during the remaining hours of the day? For then we should no longer be able to say *Give us this day* with regard to something we have already received; and it will be everyone's privilege to compel us to celebrate that Sacrament at the very last hour of the day!

27. It remains, therefore, that we should interpret " daily bread " as spiritual food, namely, the divine precepts which we are to think over and put into practice each day. It is of this that the Lord says: *Labor for the food which perisheth not.* And this food is now called " daily " as long as this temporal life goes on through days succeeding days departing. And verily as long as the disposition of the soul alternates now to the higher now to the lower, that is, now to the spiritual now to the material, much like a person who now has a good meal and again is obliged to go hungry: so long is bread a daily necessity that by it the hungry may be refreshed and the failing quickened. And thus, as our body in this life, namely, before the transformation that is to come, sensing its decline, renews itself by means of food, in like manner also

the soul, since by reason of its temporal propensities it suffers wear and tear, so to speak, in its striving after God, is restored by the food of God's precepts. Moreover, " Give us this day " was said to mean *as long as it is called today,*[57] that is, in this temporal life. Conversely, after this life we shall be fed on spiritual food forever, so that then there will be no reason to speak of " daily bread," because there the fleeting rotation of time which makes day succeed day—whence the term " today " —will not exist. But as it is said: *Today if you shall hear His voice,*[58] which the Apostle in his Epistle to the Hebrews interprets *as long as it is called today,*[59] so here, too, we should interpret " Give us *this day.*" If, however, a person chooses to take this sentence as referring also to food necessary to the body or to the Sacrament of the Lord's Body, all three ought to be taken conjointly, that is to say, in the same breath we are to ask for our daily bread—both that which is necessary for the body and the consecrated visible Bread and the invisible bread of the word of God.

CHAPTER 8

" Forgive us our debts as we also forgive our debtors ": Forgive all sins committed against you. Pecuniary debts.

28. The fifth petition follows: *And forgive us our debts as we also forgive our debtors.* That by debts sins are meant, is evident either from what the Lord Himself says: *Thou shalt not go out thence till thou repay the last farthing;* [60] or from the fact that He calls debtors those who had been reported to Him as having lost their life, some of them in the

collapse of the tower and others whose blood Herod had mingled with their sacrifice.[61] For He said that men thought these were debtors beyond measure, that is, were sinners; and He added: *I say to you, unless you do penance you shall all likewise perish.*[62] Here, therefore, it is not financial indebtedness that each is urged to remit, but to forgive whatever another has committed against him. As to debts of money, we are told to remit these by that precept rather which has been mentioned above: *If a man will contend with thee in judgment and take away thy coat, let go thy garment also unto him.*[63] Nor is it required in that passage to remit the debt to everyone who owes us money, but only to him who is so disinclined to pay it that he would rather go to court. *But the servant of the Lord,* as the Apostle says, *must not wrangle.*[64] Therefore, when a person is unwilling to pay back a debt of money either of his own accord or when notice to pay is served upon him, his debt is to be canceled. Now, his reluctance to pay will be owing to one of two reasons: either because he does not have it, or because he is miserly and covetous of another's property. In either case poverty is involved: in the former, poverty of means; in the latter, poverty of soul. Whoever, therefore, remits a debt to such a person remits it to one who is poor, and performs a Christian work with due observance of the precept to be prepared in mind to lose what is owed him. For if a person makes every effort, discreetly and calmly, to obtain repayment—bent not so much on benefitting from the money as to effect improvement [65] in a man to whom it is without doubt harmful to have the wherewithal to pay and yet not to do so—not only will he not sin, but will confer a great benefit by his endeavor to prevent the other, who is set upon making another's money his gain, from suffering the loss of his faith. And that is so much more a serious matter that there is no comparison. Hence, too, it is understood that in this fifth petition, *Forgive us our debts as we forgive our debtors*, there is no reference to money as such, but to all the things regarding which a person does us wrong; and in this reference money is included. For he sins against you who refuses to pay back money he owes you when he has the means to do so. But if you do not forgive this sin, you will not be able to say: *Forgive us as we also forgive*; and if you do forgive, you see that he who is commanded to offer such a prayer is admonished also in regard to forgiving a money debt.

29. Of course, it is possible to advance this: that when we say: *Forgive us our debts as we also forgive*, we are then convicted of acting contrary to this rule if we do not forgive those who ask our pardon while at the same time we ourselves expect our most kind Father to forgive us when we ask His pardon. But again by that precept whereby we are enjoined to pray for our enemies,[66] it is not for those who ask our pardon that we are told to pray. For surely such are not enemies. And again, it is impossible for one to say truthfully that he is praying for one whom he does not forgive. Wherefore we must own that it is incumbent on us to forgive all sins which are committed against us if we wish our Father to forgive those that we commit. As to the question of revenge, here involved, this, I think, has been sufficiently discussed above.[67]

CHAPTER 9

" Bring us not into temptation ": we must be tried,
we pray that God may not desert us in
our trial. " Deliver us from evil": that
is, from the evil of having failed in the
trial. Hope.

30. The sixth petition is: *Bring us not into temptation.*
A number of codices have " lead," which is, I think, equivalent in meaning; for both are translations of the Greek word
used, *eisenégkēs.*[68] Many when praying say: " Do not *suffer*
us to be led into temptation," evidently essaying an explanation of how the word " lead " is used.[69] God Himself does
not, of course, lead us in this, but one whom He has left
deserted of His aid He permits to be led by a most hidden
economy and by his own deserts. Often, too, it is for manifest reasons that He judges him as deserving to be thus
deserted and permits him to be led into temptation. But to
be led into temptation is one thing; to be tempted is another.
For without a trial no one can win approval, either self-
approval, as it is written: *He that hath not been tried, what*
manner of things doth he know? [70] or the approval of another,
as the Apostle says: *And your temptation in my flesh you*
despised not.[71] For it was from this that he had recognized
their steadfastness, that they had not changed their affection
for him because of the tribulations which according to the
flesh had come upon the Apostle. But to God who knows all
things before they come to pass, we are known even before
any temptation occurs.

31. Regarding, therefore, the Scripture text, *The Lord your God trieth you, that He may know if you love Him,*[72] the purpose, "that He may know," is employed for what is the actual sense, "that He may make you know," just as we speak of a "joyful day "[73] because it makes us happy; of a "numb cold "[74] because it makes us numb; and of countless things of the same sort found in our ordinary speech or in the language of scholars or in the Holy Scriptures. Failing to see this, heretics who oppose the Old Testament think that He of whom it is said: *The Lord your God trieth you,* should be branded an ignoramus; as though it were not said in the Gospel about the Lord: *And this He said to try him, for He Himself knew what He would do.*[75] Now, then, if He knew the heart of him whom He was putting to trial, what is there that He wished to see by trying him? But certainly that was done that he who was being tried might come to know himself and condemn his lack of confidence once he saw the hunger of the crowds appeased by the bread of the Lord, while he had thought that they had nothing to eat.

32. Here, therefore, the prayer is not that we be not tempted, but that we be not brought into temptation; just like a person who must undergo a trial by fire would not pray that he might not be touched by the fire, but that he might not be consumed by it.[76] *For the furnace trieth the potter's vessels, and the trial of affliction just men.*[77] Joseph therefore was tempted with the lure of adultery but he was not brought into temptation.[78] Susanna was tempted but she, too, was not led or brought into temptation;[79] and many others of both sexes, but especially Job. When those heretics and enemies of the Old Testament wish with sacrilegious mouth to mock his admirable trust in God his Lord, they air

this particularly that Satan sought permission to tempt him.[80]
For they ask of uninformed persons who can in no wise
understand these things, how Satan could talk with God.
They fail to realize, blinded as they are by superstition and
wrangling, that God does not fill place or space by any mass
of body and thus exist in one place while being absent in
another, or at least have some part here and another elsewhere; but that through the greatness of His being He is
everywhere present, not divided into parts but everywhere
complete. If they take a materialist's view of the words,
Heaven is my throne and the earth my footstool,[81] to which
passage the Lord gives witness, saying: *Swear neither by*
heaven, for it is the throne of God nor by the earth, for it is
His footstool,[82] what wonder if the devil, being placed on
earth, stood before God's feet and in His presence said
something?

When will such people grasp that there is no soul, however
perverse, but with some trace of a reasoning faculty, that has
not God speaking to its conscience? For who was it that
wrote the law of nature into the hearts of men, if not God?
It was this law concerning which the Apostle says: *For when*
the Gentiles, who have not the Law, do by nature those things
that are of the Law, these having not the Law are a law to
themselves, who show the work of the Law written in their
hearts, their conscience bearing them witness and their
thoughts between themselves accusing or also defending one
another, in the day when God shall judge the secrets of men.[83]
Wherefore, if concerning each single rational soul, even
when blinded by passion, whatever is true in its reasoning as
it thinks and reasons, must not be attributed to itself, but
to the light of truth itself by which it is enlightened, only
dimly, perhaps—according to its capacity—so as to perceive a

modicum of truth in its process of reasoning: what wonder, then, if the devil's depraved soul, perverted though it be by passion, still should be represented as having heard from the voice of God Himself, that is, from the voice of truth itself, whatever truth there was in its thoughts about a just man when it would tempt him? But whatever is false is due to that passion from which he has received the name devil.[84] And yet God has many a time spoken through the agency of a material and visible creature, sometimes to the good, sometimes to the wicked, as the Lord and Ruler of all and the Regulator of all things as the situation demanded: thus through angels who have actually been seen by human eyes, and through the Prophets, saying: "Thus saith the Lord." What wonder, then, if not by any mental process itself, but by some creature suitable for the purpose, God is said to have spoken with the devil?

33. And let them not imagine that the fact that God spoke with him constituted a recognition of dignity and, as it were, moral worth. He simply spoke to the soul of an angel though that soul was foolish and given to passion, as He might be speaking to a human soul given to folly and passion. Or let them tell us how He spoke with that rich man whose most foolish covetousness He wished to condemn, saying: *Thou fool, this night thy soul will be demanded of thee. Whose shall these things be which thou hast laid up?* [85] Certainly the Lord Himself says this in the Gospel, to which Gospel your heretics, whether they like it or not, bend their necks. But if this troubles them, that Satan should ask permission from God to tempt a just man, it is not for me to explain why this happened; but I do urge these same people to explain to me the Lord's own statement to His disciples in the Gospel: *Satan hath desired to have you, that he may sift you as*

wheat; and to Peter: *I have prayed that thy faith fail not.*[86] When they explain this to me, they will be explaining to themselves what they are asking of me. But if they cannot explain this, they must not presume to criticize brazenly in a book what they read in the Gospel without taking offense.

34. Therefore temptations come through Satan not by his power but with God's permission, either to punish men for their sins or in the plan of the Lord's mercy to put them on probation and trial. Moreover, it makes a very great difference into what sort of temptation the individual falls. For example, Judas who sold his Master did not fall into one of the same nature as Peter who by an obsession of fear denied Him. There are temptations that are but human, I believe, when a person, though meaning well, yet through human frailty fails to live up to some resolve or becomes irritated with a brother in his zeal to correct him, going just a little beyond the limits set him by Christian composure. Concerning such the Apostle says: *Let no temptation take hold on you but such as is human*; while he also says: *And God is faithful, who would not let you be tempted above that which you are able, but will also make with temptation issue that you may be able to bear it.*[87] By this statement he quite clearly shows that we are not to pray that we may not be tempted, but that we may not be led into temptations. For we are led into them if they are such as we cannot endure. But when dangerous temptations, into which it is our undoing to be brought and led, arise from either temporal fortune or misfortune, no one is broken down by the visitation of adversity who does not succumb to the lure of prosperity.

35. The seventh and last petition is: *But deliver us from evil.* We must pray not only that we may not be led into

the evil from which we are free—which is asked for in the sixth place—but that we may also be delivered from the evil into which we have already been led. And when this has been accomplished, nothing will remain to inspire dread nor will any temptation at all have to be dreaded. And yet in this life, as long as we are bearers of this mortality into which we were led by the inducement of the serpent, there is no hope of accomplishing this. But that it will be accomplished some day is a hope that should be entertained; and this is the hope which is not seen, whereof when the Apostle discussed it he said: *But hope that is seen is not hope.*[88] Yet the wisdom which is granted in this life also, is not to be despaired of by the faithful servants of God. And it is this—that with the utmost care we shun what from the Lord's revelation we know we must avoid and that with a most intense devotion we strive after what from God's revelation we know we should strive after. For thus when death itself slips from us the last burden of our mortality in our appointed time, the blessedness of the whole man will be brought to pass, a blessedness that was begun in this life and which to grasp and attain some day we now expend every effort.

CHAPTER 10

The Lord's Prayer is divided into two groups of petitions. The temporal and the eternal as distinguishing marks.

36. Now, the points of difference in these seven petitions deserve consideration and special mention. Thus, our present life is being spent now—for a time, while the life we hope

for is eternal. Again, eternal things are of supreme worth; still it is only when we have done with the temporal, that we make the exchange of the other. The accomplishment of the first three petitions, it is true, begins with the present life, the life that is spent in this world. For the sanctification of God's name began with the moment of the Lord's lowly coming; [89] again, the coming of His kingdom in which He will come in glory will be manifested not after the end of the world, but in the end of the world; and again, the perfect doing of His will as in heaven so on earth—whether you take heaven and earth to mean the just and the sinners, or the spirit and the flesh, or the Lord and the Church, or all these things taken together—will be brought about in the moment that our blessedness is made perfect, that is to say, at the end of the world. Yet all three are to continue for eternity. For the sanctification of God's name will go on without end and there will be no end to His kingdom; and everlasting life is promised in our state of perfect blessedness. Therefore those three things will abide in their consummate plenitude in that life which is promised to us.

37. But the four remaining petitions seem to me to relate to our present life. The first of these is, *Give us this day our daily bread.* By the very fact that it is called " *daily* bread " whether this is meant as something spiritual or as something visible, either in the Sacrament or that which now keeps us alive, it pertains to the present time which He has called " this day." Not that spiritual food is not everlasting; but because that which is called daily food in Scripture is represented to the soul either through the sound of speech or some signs of the temporal order—things all of which certainly will not exist when all will be *taught of God* [90] and will not merely

give intimation of truth by the activities of their body, but drink in its ineffable light itself by the purity of their mind.

Perhaps it was for this reason, too, that bread, not drink, was mentioned, because bread is converted into nourishment only by breaking and chewing it just as Scripture feeds the soul by being opened up and discussed; but drink is already prepared, passes as it is into the body. Thus in the present time truth is bread, speaking as we do of daily bread; but then it will be drink when there will be no need of laborious discussions and disputations—as it were, of breaking and chewing—but only of drinking the clear, limpid waters of truth.

And it is now that our sins are forgiven and now that we forgive, which is the second of these four remaining petitions; but in the next life there will be no pardon of sins because there will be no sins. And temptations beset this present life, but they will not exist when that which is written is perfected: *Thou shalt hide them in the secret of Thy face.*[91] And the evil from which we wish to be delivered and the deliverance from evil itself certainly have to do with this life, whose mortality we have deserved through the justice of God and from which we are freed by His mercy.

CHAPTER 11

Seven Gifts, seven Beatitudes, seven petitions. Our contract with God.

38. It seems to me that this number seven [92] which attaches to these petitions corresponds to the number seven from which this whole sermon began. For if it is the fear of

the Lord [93] through which the poor in spirit are blessed, *because theirs is the kingdom of heaven,* let us pray that *the name* of God *may be hallowed* among men through *holy fear enduring for ever and ever.*[94]

If it is through piety that the meek are blessed, *because they will inherit the land,* let us pray that His *kingdom will come,* whether it be upon ourselves that we may become meek and not resist Him, or whether it be from heaven to earth in the bright glory of the Lord's coming in which we shall rejoice and be commended, with Him saying: *Come, ye blessed of my Father; possess you the kingdom prepared for you from the foundation of the world.*[95] For, says the Prophet: *In the Lord shall my soul be praised; let the meek hear and rejoice.*[96]

If it is through knowledge that those who mourn are blessed, *because they will be comforted,* let us pray that His *will be done on earth as it is in heaven,* because when the body—the earth—will be in accord with the spirit—heaven—in supreme and perfect peace, we shall not grieve. For really in this present time there is no other grief but that which rises when these are in conflict with each other and compel us to say: *I see another law in my members, fighting against the law of my mind;* and to testify our grief with tearful voice: *Unhappy man that I am, who shall deliver me from the body of this death?* [97]

If it is through fortitude that those who hunger and thirst after justice are blessed, *because they shall have their fill,* let us pray that *our daily bread be given us this day,* in the strength and support of which we can come to that fullest abundance.

If it is through counsel that the merciful are blessed, *because they shall obtain mercy,* let us *forgive our debtors* their debts and let us pray that *ours be forgiven us.*

If it is through understanding that the clean of heart are blessed, *because they shall see God*, let us pray that we *be not led into temptation*, lest we have a divided heart in not seeking the one good to which we should refer all we do, but at the same time pursuing the temporal and earthly. For temptations in those matters which seem to men grave and direful will prove powerless in us, if those other temptations have no power over us which come through the enticements of the things which are associated by men with goodness and happiness.

If it is through wisdom that the peacemakers are blessed, *because they shall be called the children of God*, let us pray that we *be delivered from evil*, for that deliverance will make us children, that is, sons of God, so that in the spirit of adoption we may cry *Abba, Father*.[98]

39. Surely, we must not indifferently pass over the fact that of all those texts in which the Lord has commanded us to pray, He declared that special emphasis should be laid on the petition which has to do with the forgiveness of sins. In it He wished us to show commiseration, the one and only counsel for avoiding misery. For in no other text do we pray in such a way that we, as it were, enter a contract with God, saying as we do: *Forgive us as we also forgive*. If we lie in that contract, the whole prayer has no value. For he has this to say: *For if you will forgive men their offenses, your Father who is in heaven will forgive you also. But if you will not forgive men, neither will your Father forgive you your offenses* (14 f.).

CHAPTER 12

Fasting.

40. There follows a precept about fasting which has to do with that same cleansing of the heart now under discussion. For in this work, too, a person must take heed that no spirit of self-display creeps in, no craving for human applause, which divides the heart and prevents it from being pure and candid for acquiring knowledge of God. *And when you fast,* He says, *be not as the hypocrites, sad. For they disfigure their face that they may appear unto men to fast. Amen, I say to you, they have received their reward. But you, when you fast, anoint your heads and wash your faces that you appear not to men to fast but to your Father who is in secret; and your Father who seeth in secret will repay you* (16-18). It is evident from these precepts that our entire striving is to be directed towards inward joys, to keep ourselves from seeking outward rewards and becoming conformed to this world and forfeiting the promise of a blessedness which is the more solid and enduring as it is interior, and by which God chose us *to be made conformable to the image of His Son.*[99]

41. But in this section particular attention must be given to the fact that there can be ostentation not only amid the splendor and pomp of material things but, also in the drab of sackcloth itself; and this is all the more dangerous as it masquerades in the guise of service to God. Thus, when a person is loudly conspicuous by an extravagant care of the body and by a display of clothes or other things, there is no question

but that these very things stamp him a worldling and that he deceives no one if he puts on an air of sanctimoniousness. But as to a person who in making profession of his Christianity draws the eyes of people to himself by his extraordinary show of sackcloth and ashes: when he does this of his own accord and not under the duress of necessity, it can be gathered from the rest of his behavior whether he does this from contempt of care that can be dispensed with, or merely to make an impression. Here also the Lord tells us to beware of wolves under a sheep's skin: *By their fruits*, He said, *you shall know them.*[100] For when by some situations those very things are being taken away or denied which they have realized or wish to realize in this guise, then of necessity it becomes apparent whether he is a wolf in a sheep's skin or a sheep in its own. On the other hand, a Christian must not intrigue the eyes of men by his elaborate dress simply because frauds, too, only too often put on other dress—that which serves bare necessity—to deceive the unwary: plainly, such sheep, too, must not lay aside their own skins merely because at times wolves use the same to cover themselves.

42. Hence the common question, what is meant by His statement: *But you, when you fast, anoint your heads and wash your faces that you appear not to men to fast.* For certainly a person would not be in the right, were he, while we do have the every-day practice of washing our face, to prescribe that we ought also to have our hair anointed when we fast. Granting that all find this most objectionable, the necessary conclusion is that this precept of oiling the hair and washing the face refers to the interior man. Now, then, putting oil on the head refers to joy; washing the face, to cleanness; and therefore a person anoints his head when he rejoices within, in his mind and reason. As to the head, we

are right in regarding it as that which has the pre-eminence in the soul and by which all else that concerns man is governed and controlled. And he does this who does not seek joy from without for the purpose of realizing the joy of the flesh in human praise. For the flesh, which ought to be subordinated, is in no way the head of the whole man. *No one* indeed *ever hated his own flesh*,[101] as the Apostle says in stating the precept about loving one's wife; *and the head of the woman is the man,* and of the man Christ is the head.[102]

In his fasting, therefore, let a man rejoice inwardly in the very fact that by this his fasting he is turning away from the pleasures of the world to make himself subject to Christ, who in the words of this precept wants him to have his head anointed. With the same intent he will be washing his face, that is, cleansing his heart whereby he is to see God, with no veil intervening because of a beclouding infirmity—firm and unshaken because he is clean and upright. *Wash yourselves,* He said, *be clean. Take away the iniquities from your souls and from the sight of my eyes.*[103] From this filth, then, our face must be washed, the filth that offends the eyes of God. For *we, beholding the glory of the Lord with open face, ·shall be transformed into the same image.*[104]

43. Often, too, reflection upon the things we need for carrying on this life injures the eye of our spirit and bedims it; and for the most part it divides our heart, so that in the things which to all appearances we do rightly in our relations with our fellow men, we actually fail to do them with the intention the Lord demands, that is, not because we love them, but merely because we wish to obtain some advantage from them in view of the needs of the present life. But we ought to do good to them motivated by their eternal welfare, not by some temporal concern of our own. May God, there-

fore, incline our heart to His testimonies and not to gain.[105]
For *the end of the commandment is charity from a pure heart,
a good conscience, and an unfeigned faith.*[106] He who looks
after the interests of a brother with a view to his own needs
in this life, certainly is not acting in a spirit of love; for he
is not looking after the interests of one whom he ought to love
as he loves himself, but after his own; or rather, not even
after his own, since he is thus making his heart a divided
heart and so preventing himself from seeing God, in the
vision of whom alone is certain and lasting blessedness.

CHAPTER 13

The right intention is all-important.

44. Logically, therefore, in His insistence on the cleansing of our heart He continues and prescribes, saying: *Lay
not up to yourselves treasures on earth where moth and rust
destroy and where thieves break through and steal. But lay
up to yourselves treasures in heaven where neither moth nor
rust doth destroy and where thieves do not break through nor
steal. For where thy treasure is, there will be thy heart also*
(19-21).[107] Therefore, if one's heart is on the earth, that is,
if a person does anything with his heart set on gaining a
material advantage, how will that heart be clean, wallowing
as it does on the earth? But if it is in heaven, it will be
clean, because whatsoever has to do with heaven is clean. A
thing becomes adulterated when it is mixed with something
inferior, however pure that other thing may be of itself. Thus
gold is adulterated even by pure silver, when mixed with it.
So also our soul becomes tarnished through our desire for

the things of the earth, though the earth itself is clean in its own nature and level.

However, in this passage I would not take heaven as corporeal, because whatever is corporeal should be regarded as earth. For he who lays up treasures for himself in heaven ought to ignore the whole world. We must, therefore, set up and place our treasure and our heart in that heaven about which it is written: *The heaven of heaven is the Lord's*,[108] that is to say, in the spiritual firmament—not in the heaven that is to pass away, but in that which abides forever; for *heaven and earth shall pass*.[109]

45. And here He makes clear that He is giving all these precepts for the cleansing of our hearts, when He says: *The light of thy body is thy eye. If therefore thy eye be single, thy whole body shall be lightsome. But if thy eye be evil, thy whole body shall be darksome. If then the light that is in thee be darkness, the darkness itself how great shall it be* (22 f.)! This passage is to be understood thus: that we shall know all our works are clean and pleasing in the sight of God if they are done with a single heart, that is, with that supernal intention whose end is love; *for love is the fulfilling of the law*.[110] The " eye," therefore, we ought to take as meaning in this place the intention by which we do whatever we do. If it is clean and upright and keeping in view what it ought to keep in view, all our works which we perform in accordance with it are necessarily good. All such works He designated as the " whole body "; for the Apostle, too, speaks of certain works as our members which he reproves and requires us to mortify, saying: *Mortify therefore your members which are upon the earth: fornication, uncleanness, . . . covetousness*, and the other things of this kind.[111]

46. Therefore not what one does, but with what intention he does it, is the thing to consider. For this is the "light" within us, because it is by this that we are certain of doing with a good intent what we are doing; *for all that is made manifest is light.*[112] The deeds themselves which we perform and which affect human society have an uncertain issue; and therefore He called them "darkness." When, for instance, I give money to a poor person who asks for it, I do not know what he will do with it or suffer from it. It may happen that he does some evil with it or suffers some evil because of it— a thing which I did not wish to happen when I gave it, nor would I have given it with that intention. If, therefore, I did it with a good intention and I was conscious of this as I did it, and hence this is called "light": then, whatever may be the outcome, my deed is also done in the light; but the outcome, because it is uncertain and unknown, is called darkness. If, however, I did it with a bad intention, even the light itself it darkness. For in this we speak of light because each one knows with what motivation he acts even when he acts with a bad motive; but the light itself is darkness because the intention is not directed undivided to things above, but is deflected to things below and through the heart's duplicity it casts, as it were, a shadow. *If, then, the light that is in thee be darkness, the darkness itself how great shall it be!*—that is, if the very intention of your heart, by which you do what you do and of which you are conscious, is tarnished by a craving for earthly and temporal things and as a result blinded, how much more is the action whose outcome uncertain, tarnished and enveloped in darkness! For, even though what you do with an intention which is not upright and pure may turn out well for someone, it is how you have done it, not how it has turned out for him, that is imputed to you.

CHAPTER 14

No one can serve two masters.

47. Now, what He says next, *No man can serve two masters*, is to be referred to the intention we have been discussing; and this He further explains, saying: *for either he will hate the one and love the other, or he will sustain the one and despise the other.* These words must receive careful attention; for example, who the two masters are He shows next, saying: *You cannot serve God and mammon* (24). Among the Hebrews riches are said to be called " mammon." There is also the corresponding Punic term: " profit " in Punic is called " mammon." [113] Now, anyone serving mammon serves him indeed who, placed over these worldly things in tribute to his wickedness, is called by the Lord *the ruler of this world*.[114] A man, therefore, *either will hate* this one *and love the other*, namely God, *or he will sustain the one and despise the other.* Whoever serves mammon delivers himself over to a master harsh and malignant; caught by his own cupidity, he puts himself under the devil, yet does not love him; for who is there who loves the devil? And nevertheless he submits to him: as when on some large estate a man is attached to the slave girl of another, he endures harsh servitude because of his passion of love, even if he does not care for him whose slave he loves.

48. But *he will despise the other*, He has said; not, " he will hate him." For scarcely anyone's conscience permits him to hate God; [115] but ignore Him he will—that is, he does not fear Him; as it were, he takes His goodness for granted. From this indifference and baneful overconfidence the Holy

Spirit calls us away when He says through the Prophet: *Son, add not sin upon sin; and say not, " The mercy of God is great ";* [116] and, *Knowest thou not that the patience of God inviteth thee to penance?* [117] Can anyone be mentioned whose mercy is such as His who forgives penitents all their sins and makes the wild olive *partaker of the fatness of the olive tree,* but whose severity is so great as His *who hath not spared the natural branches,* but *because of unbelief broke them off?* [118] But whoever wishes to love God and to take care not to offend Him, must not think that he can serve two masters; and let him keep the intention of his heart straight and free from any entanglement in duplicity. In this way he will *think of the Lord in goodness and seek Him in simplicity of heart.* [119]

CHAPTER 15

We are in God's care. The evident lesson.

49. Therefore, He said, *I say to you, be not solicitous for your life, what you shall eat, nor for your body, what you shall put on* (25). Even though our seeking may not be after unnecessary things, still the chance must not be taken of having a divided heart in respect to necessities themselves and of having our intention turned aside to a seeking of our own interests when we do something that looks like an act of mercy—that is, of wishing to appear to be looking after the interests of someone while actually attending to our own gain rather than to his advantage; and we might not think ourselves to be sinning for the reason that what we are after is something necessary, not superfluous. But the Lord ad-

monishes us to remember that God in creating us and fitting us with a body and soul has given us far more than food and clothing, for the care of which He does not want us to make our heart a divided heart. *Is not*, He says, *the life more than the meat?* Thus you are to understand that He who gave us life will much more easily give us meat. *And the body more than the raiment* (25)—that is, it is more. Similarly you are to understand that He who gave the body will much more easily give raiment.

50. In this passage it is frequently asked whether the food mentioned has reference to the soul,[120] since the soul is immaterial and the food spoken of is material. But here let us take for granted that the word "soul" stands for "life" whose support is that material nourishment. It is also with this import that the word is used in the remark: *He that loveth his life shall lose it.*[121] Unless we take this to mean the present life which we must sacrifice for the kingdom of God, as evidently the martyrs were strong enough to do, this precept will be contrary to that statement whereby it was said: *What doth it profit a man if he gain the whole world, and lose his own soul?* [122]

51. *Behold the birds of the air, for they neither sow nor do they reap nor gather into barns; and your heavenly Father feedeth them. Are not you of more value than they* (26)? Actually, you are more valuable. For without doubt a rational being such as man is, ranks higher in nature than the irrational ones, such as birds. *And which of you by taking thought can add to his stature one cubit? And for raiment why are you solicitous* (27 f.)? That is to say, the providence of Him by whose power and sway it has come about that your body was brought to its present stature, can also clothe

it. That it was not brought about by your solicitude that your body reached its present stature can be recognized from this, that if you were anxious and wished to add a cubit to your height, you could not. Therefore, leave to Him the care also of clothing your body by whose care you see it brought about that you have a body of such a stature.

52. But there had to be also an illustration in the matter of clothing as there had been in regard to food; therefore, He goes on to say: *Consider the lilies of the field, how they grow; they labor not neither do they spin, but I say to you that not even Solomon in all his glory was arrayed as one of these. And if the grass of the field, which is today and to-morrow is cast into the oven, God doth so clothe how much more therefore you, O ye of little faith* (28-30)? Now, these illustrations must not be treated as allegories so that we should ask ourselves what birds of the air and lilies of the field mean: they have been introduced here for the simple reason that from unimportant things an important lesson might be forced home; just as is the case of the judge [123] *who feared not God nor regarded man,* but yet yielded to the widow who often importuned him to consider her case—not through any kindly or humane sentiments, but to keep her from bothering him. But in no way can that unjust judge represent God's person allegorically; and yet, how much God, good and just as He is, cares for those who implore His mercy, the Lord wished to be inferred from this, that not even a wicked man can ignore those who ply him with insistent pleas, even though it is only to avoid annoyance.

CHAPTER 16

Living for the Gospel. Preaching it as sons, not as slaves.

53. *Be not solicitous, therefore, saying, "What shall we eat?" or, "Wherewith shall we be clothed?" For after all these things do the heathens seek. For your Father knoweth that you have need of all these things. Seek ye, therefore, first the kingdom of God and His justice, and all these things will be added unto you* (31-33). Here He most clearly shows that these things are not to be sought after as though the goodness that we have in them were such that because of them we must do well in whatever we do; though they are necessary. The difference between a good that must be sought and something that we must of necessity take to use, He declared in this sentence when He said: *Seek ye first the kingdom of God and His justice and all these things will be added unto you.* The kingdom of God therefore and His justice are our good, and this must be sought and that must be the end we have in view in doing whatever we do. But because in this life we serve as soldiers in order that we may be able to reach that kingdom, and this life cannot be lived without these necessary things, He says: *these things will be added unto you;* but for your part, *seek ye first the kingdom of God and His justice.* For in using the word "first" for the latter He indicated that the former are to be sought later, not in point of time, but of worth; the one as our good, the other as something necessary for us and necessary in view of that good.

54. To illustrate: we ought not to preach the Gospel for the reason that we may eat; but we should eat so that we may preach the Gospel. If we preach so that we can eat, we evidently think less of the Gospel than food, and our good will consist merely in our eating, and what we cannot dispense with will be our preaching. The Apostle, moreover, forbids this when he declares that it is indeed his right and a concession granted by the Lord to those who preach the Gospel, to live by the Gospel: [124] that is, they should have from the Gospel those things that are necessary for this life; but that he had not availed himself of this right. For there were many who wished for an occasion to get and sell the Gospel, and to cut these off from such occasion, the Apostle supported himself by his own hands.[125] It is concerning such that he says in another place: *that I may cut off the occasion from them that desire occasion.*[126] Although even if, like the other good Apostles, with Our Lord's permission he had lived by the Gospel, he would not therefore have made his livelihood the motive of his preaching but rather based his living on the Gospel, that is, as I have said above, his purpose in preaching would not have been to obtain food and whatever other indispensable things there are; but he would have availed himself of these things in order that he might do justice to that other object, and not preach the Gospel against his will because necessity forced him.

This is what he reproves when he says: *Know you not that they who work in the holy place eat the things that are of the holy place; and they that serve the altar partake of the altar? So also the Lord ordained that they who preach the Gospel should live by the Gospel. But I have used none of these things.*[127] Hence he shows that it was allowed, not commanded; otherwise he stands convicted of having acted contrary to the Lord's command. Then he goes on to say: *Neither have I written these things, that they should be so done unto me; for it is good for me to die rather than that any man should make my glory void.*[128] This he said because, noting those who were seeking an occasion, he had already determined to gain his livelihood by his own hands. *For if I preach the Gospel,* he says, *it is no glory to me:* [129] that is, if my motive for preaching the Gospel is that such things may materialize in my case—in other words, if I preach the Gospel that I may get these things and so place the purpose of the Gospel in food and drink and clothing. But why is it no glory to him? *For a necessity lieth upon me,*[130] he says; that is, I should then be preaching to gain a temporal advantage from preaching eternal things; for then dire need binds me to the Gospel, not my will. *For woe is unto me,* he says, *if I preach not the Gospel.*[131]

But how ought he to preach the Gospel? Why, in such a manner as to put his reward in the Gospel itself and in the kingdom of God. Thus he can preach the Gospel not by compulsion, but because he wills to do so. *For if I do this thing willingly,* he says, *I have a reward; but if against my will, a dispensation is committed to me;* [132] that is, if compelled by a lack of those things which are necessary for this temporal life I preach the Gospel, others through me will have the reward of the Gospel. They will love the Gospel because of my preaching it; but I shall not have that reward because it is not the Gospel itself I love, but the compensation it brings me in the form of those temporal things. And this is an outrage that we should find anyone ministering the Gospel not as a son, but merely as a slave to whom this has been given as a commission; that he should pass it on, so to speak, as something that does not concern him and receive nothing more for his service than victuals, given to him not for his sharing in the kingdom, but from an outside source for the sustenance of his wretched servitude. Still, in another place he says that he is also a dispenser.[183] For even a slave once adopted into the family as a son can in all loyalty dispense to those who share with him that which has fallen to him as joint heir with them. But in the present case where he says: *But if against my will, a dispensation is committed to me,* he wished such a dispenser to be understood as one who dispenses something that does not concern him and from which he himself receives nothing.

55. Hence, whatever is sought on account of something else is unquestionably inferior to that because of which it is sought; and therefore that is first on account of which you seek a given thing, not that thing which you seek because of something else. It follows that if we seek the Gospel and the kingdom of God because of food, we give priority to the food and relegate the kingdom to the second place; so that if there were no lack of food, we would not seek the kingdom of God. This is to seek food first and then the kingdom of God, that is, to put the former in first place, the latter, in second place. But if we seek food in order to gain the kingdom of God, we are doing what was said: *Seek ye first the kingdom of God and His justice and all these things will be added unto you.*

CHAPTER 17

In the service of our country—the kingdom of God.

56. If we seek first the kingdom of God and His justice, if, therefore, we put this before everything else, so that it is because of it that we seek the other things, we should not be concerned that we may not have the things that we need in this life in view of God's kingdom. For He said above: *Your Father knoweth that you have need of all these things.* And therefore when He had said: *Seek ye first the kingdom of God and His justice,* He did not say: "Then seek these other things"—though they are necessary; but He said: *All these things will be added unto you,* that is, they will follow as a matter of course if you seek the other without running foul of yourselves. You are not to be diverted from the former by seeking the latter. Or, in other words, you are not to have two objectives: you are not to seek both the kingdom of God for its own sake and these necessary things; but these rather for the sake of the other. Do this, and you will not lack them. For you cannot serve two masters. But a man does try to serve two masters if he seeks both the kingdom of God for the great good it is and also those other temporal things. He will not be able to keep his eye undivided and serve the Lord God alone unless he takes all other things so far as they are necessary because of this one single object, namely, the kingdom of God.

And just as all in military service receive rations and pay, so all who preach the Gospel receive food and raiment. But not all who serve as soldiers do so for the welfare of the country but for what they get. So, too, not all are ministers of God for the welfare of the Church, but for the temporal things which they stand to realize—their provisions and pay, as it were; or it is for both, the one and the other. But it was already said above: *You cannot serve two masters.* Therefore, with undivided heart we should work good to all solely because of the kingdom of God; and in so doing we should not have our minds either on the temporal reward alone or as conjoined with God's kingdom.

For all these temporal goods He has used the word " tomorrow," saying: *Take no thought of tomorrow.*[134] Now, the word " tomorrow " is not used except in speaking of time where the future follows upon the past. Therefore, when we do any sort of good, let us not think of the temporal but of the eternal; then our work will be good and perfect. *For the morrow will be solicitous for itself:* that is to say, when it will be time for you to take food or drink or put on clothing— in other words, when necessity itself begins to press you. These things, we may be sure, will be at hand because our Father knows that we have need of all these things. *For,* so He says, *sufficient for the day is the evil thereof* (34); that is, it suffices that necessity itself will urge us to take such things. And that this has been called an evil is, I suppose, because for us it is a punishment; for it has to do with this frailty and mortality which we have merited by sinning.[135] Hence, to this punishment of temporal necessity do not add an additional burden; you will then not only patiently bear the want of such things, but will also for the purpose of satisfying this want serve as a soldier of God.

57. Here, however, we must be scrupulously on our guard; or it may happen that when we see some servant of God providing against a lack of those necessary things either for himself or for those committed to his charge, we judge

him to be acting against the precept of the Lord and to be solicitous for the morrow. Even the Lord Himself, let us remember, to whom angels ministered [186]—setting an example that no one might afterwards take scandal when he observed any of His servants procuring such necessaries—found it proper to have purses with money to serve whatever needs might turn up; of which purses Judas, who betrayed Him, was the custodian and thief.[187] So, too, the Apostle Paul may appear to have taken thought for the morrow when he said: *Now, concerning the collections for the saints, as I have given order to the churches of Galatia, so do ye also. On the first day of the week let every one of you put apart with himself, laying up what it shall please him; that when I come, the collections be not then to be made. And when I shall come, whomsoever you shall approve by letters, them I will send to carry your grace to Jerusalem. And if it is meet that I also go, they shall go with me. Now I will come to you when I shall have passed through Macedonia. For I shall pass through Macedonia. And with you I shall abide, or even spend the winter, that you may bring me on my way whithersoever I shall go. For I will not see you now by the way; for I trust that I shall abide with you some time, if the Lord permit. But I will tarry at Ephesus until Pentecost.*[188] Likewise in the Acts of the Apostles it is recorded that in the face of impending famine the necessaries of life were provided against the future. For so we read: *And in those days there came prophets from Jerusalem to Antioch, and there was great rejoicing. And when we were together in assembly, one of them, named Agabus, rising up, signified by the Spirit that there should be a great famine over the whole world, which came to pass under Claudius Caesar. And of the disciples, as each had it in his power, everyone of them pur-*

posed to send relief to the presbyters for the brethren who dwelt in Judea, who also sent it by the hand of Barnabas and Saul.[139] Again, as the same Apostle Paul was going to sea, and provisions that were offered were brought on board for him, the food furnished, so it seems, was not for just one day.[140] And when the same writes again: *He that stole, let him now steal no more; but rather let him labor, working with his hands the thing which is good, that he may have something to give to him that has need,*[141] those who misunderstand him think that he is not observing the precept of the Lord wherein He says: *Behold the birds of the air, for they neither sow nor do they reap nor gather into barns;* and, *Consider the lilies of the field, how they grow; they labor not neither do they spin;* while he is commanding them to labor, working with their hands, so that they may have something which they can give to others also. And, noting as we do that he often says of himself that he worked with his own hands so as not to be a burden to anyone,[142] and it is written of him that he associated himself with Aquila because they were brother craftsmen,[143] that working together they might provide their livelihood, he does not seem to have imitated the birds of the air and the lilies of the field.

From these and like passages in Scripture it is amply apparent that the Lord did not disapprove the procuring of these things in the way men ordinarily do; but only when one would be a soldier of God for the sake of these things, so as to be guided in his efforts not by the kingdom of God, but by the acquisition of such things.

58. This whole precept, then, reduces itself to this rule of life, that even while providing for such things we should keep our minds on the kingdom of God, but in the service of God's kingdom we should not think of them. For thus, even

if at times these things should be lacking—a situation which God frequently allows for our own training—this not only does not cripple our resolution, but even makes it stronger by the trial and test it receives. For, he said, *we glory in tribulation, knowing that tribulation worketh patience; and patience trial; and trial hope; and hope confoundeth not, because the charity of God is poured forth in our hearts by the Holy Ghost who is given to us.*[144] And in recalling his tribulations and labors, the same Apostle mentions that he has labored not only in prison and shipwreck and many a similar trouble, but also in hunger and thirst, in cold and nakedness.[145]

When we read this, let us not come to the conclusion that the Lord's promises have proved insecure and that to the extent that the Apostle endured hunger and thirst and nakedness while seeking the kingdom of God and His justice, whereas it was said to us: *Seek ye first the kingdom of God and His justice and all these things will be added unto you*: because that Physician, to whom we have given ourselves without reserve and from whom we have the promise of the present life and the future, knows that such things are so many helps [146] to us when He brings them on or takes them away as He judges most helpful for us, whom He rules and directs through consolation and trial in this life and after this life will firmly establish in everlasting rest. Indeed man, too, when he frequently takes away the fodder from his beast of burden, is not depriving it of his care; rather, because he is caring for it, he does what he is doing.

CHAPTER 18

Leave judgment to God. Rash judgment.

59. And because it is uncertain what motivation lies behind the gathering of such things for future use or of holding them in reserve if use does not claim them, since the gathering can proceed from a single heart as it can from a divided heart, He appositely added at this point: *Judge not, that you may not be judged. For with what judgment you judge, you shall be judged; and with what measure you mete, it shall be measured to you again* (7. 1 f.). I think this text enjoins on us this one thing: that in the case of those actions whose motivation is in doubt, we are to put the better construction on them. In the passage, *By their fruits you shall know them*,[147] the statement has to do with things which manifestly cannot be done with a good intention, such as lewd actions or blasphemies or thefts or drunkenness and all such things concerning which we are permitted to pass judgment, the Apostle saying: *For what have I to do to judge them that are without? Do not you judge them that are within?* [148]

In the matter of foods, since any sort of human food can be taken indifferently with upright intention and sincere heart without involving the vice of concupiscence, the same Apostle forbids judgment to be passed on such as ate flesh meat and drank wine by those who abstained from such foods. *Let not him that eateth despise him that eateth not; and he that eateth not let him not judge him that eateth.* There he also says: *Who art thou that judgest another man's servant? To his own lord he standeth or falleth.*[149] In matters such as these which can be done with an upright and single-hearted and magnanimous intention—though the opposite of a good intention is also possible—the persons referred to wished, though they were mere men, to pass judgment upon the secrets of the heart, of which God alone is judge.

60. Related to this is what he says in another place: *Judge nothing before the time until the Lord come who will both bring to light the hidden things of darkness and will make manifest the counsels of the hearts; and then shall every man have praise from God.*[150] So, there are some actions that are neutral, regarding which we do not know with what intention they are done, because they may be done both with a good or with a bad one and it is rash to judge of them, especially if the verdict is condemnatory. The time will come when such actions will pass under judgment, when *the Lord will bring to light the hidden things of darkness and will make manifest the counsels of the hearts.* The same Apostle says the same elsewhere: *Some men's sins are manifest, going before to judgment; and some men they follow after.*[151] They are " manifest," he says, because it is clear what motivation prompts them; these " are going before to judgment," that is, if judgment is made after their commission, the judgment will not be a rash one; but those which are concealed " follow after," because neither will they be concealed in their own time. A like notion obtains for good actions, for he goes on to add: *In like manner also good deeds are manifest; and they that are otherwise cannot be hid.*[152] Let us, therefore, judge only with respect to what is manifest, but leave to God's judgment what is hidden; because this, too, cannot be hidden, be it good or bad, when the time comes for it to be made manifest.

61. Now, there are two situations in which we must guard

against rash judgment: when it is uncertain why and with what disposition a thing is done; or when it is uncertain what sort of person he will be who now appears to be either good or bad. Suppose, for example, someone alleges stomach trouble as the reason for his not wishing to fast; and you, not believing it, attribute it to his weakness for glutting himself with food: you would be passing a rash judgment. Again, if you found him obviously glutting and inebriating himself and you then passed censure on him as one beyond all possibility of any change for the better, you would yet pass a rash judgment. Let us not, therefore, pass condemnatory judgment in matters whose motivation we do not know; nor let us decry the obvious as if despairing of a remedy; and thus we shall avoid the judgment of which it is here said: *Judge not, that you may not be judged.*

62. But there may be some confusion over His statement: *For with what judgment you judge, you shall be judged; and with what measure you mete, it shall be measured to you again.* Can it be, then, that if we give expression to a judgment that is rash, God will also judge us rashly? Or if we measure with an unjust measure, that in God's case too, there is in store an unjust measure by which it shall be measured to us again? For, I take it, the judgment itself is meant by the word " measure."

No, not at all. God neither judges rashly nor does He requite with an unjust measure. But the force of the statement is that the very same rashness with which you penalize another must rebound upon you. Unless perhaps we are to suppose that injustice should somehow do harm to him against whom it is directed but in no way to him from whom it proceeds! No—often enough no harm is done at all to him who suffers an injustice, whereas the one who perpetrates it cannot help being harmed. Did any harm come to the martyrs from the injustice of their persecutors? [153] No; but to the persecutors—yes, and in very great measure. Because, though some of them changed their ways, yet at the time they were persecuting, their malice blinded them.

Thus frequently a rash judgment does no harm to him who is the object of the rash judgment, but the one who makes such a judgment cannot but suffer harm from his rashness. By this norm, I think, the following was also said: *All that use the sword shall perish with the sword.*[154] How many there are who use the sword, yet do not perish by the sword, as neither did Peter himself! But lest someone think that because he had received forgiveness of his sins, therefore he escaped such a form of punishment—though nothing could be more absurd than to think that the punishment of the sword, which did not befall Peter, could have been greater than that of the cross, which did befall him: [155] what is he going to say about the robbers who were crucified with the Lord,[156] seeing that the one who merited pardon merited it after he had been crucified, while the other merited no pardon whatever? Could it be that they had crucified all whom they had killed and therefore deserved to suffer crucifixion themselves? It is ridiculous to think that What other meaning, therefore, attaches to the statement, *All that take the sword shall perish with the sword*, but that the soul is killed by the presence of sin, whatever it may be which it has committed?

CHAPTER 19

*The mote and the beam: look to yourself, see your-
self in the weakness of another.*

63. And, because the Lord in this passage is warning us
against rash and unjust judgments—for He wishes that whatever we do we should do with an undivided heart and with a
heart intent upon God alone; and because there is no certainty with regard to the intention with which many things
are done and to pass judgment on them is rash; and because
those most of all judge rashly and are quick to criticize respecting uncertain matters who love to censure and condemn
rather than correct and amend, which fault stems either from
pride or from jealousy: therefore it was logical for Him to
add, saying: *And why seest thou the mote that is in thy
brother's eye, but seest not the beam that is in thy own eye*
(3)? Thus, if he, for example, sinned through anger and
you were to reprove him in hatred: there would be, so to
speak, just as much difference between anger and hatred as
there is between a mote and a beam. For hatred is inveterate
anger which, as it were, by the mere fact of its long duration
has taken on such strength that it deservedly is called a
" beam." Again, it is quite possible that in becoming angry
with a person you actually wish for his amendment; however,
if you hate a person, you cannot wish to change him for the
better.

64. *For how sayest thou to thy brother: " Let me cast the
mote out of thy eye," and behold a beam is in thy own eye?
Thou hypocrite, cast out first the beam out of thy own eye,*

and then thou shalt see to cast the mote out of thy brother's eye (4 f.). That is, first get rid of your hatred and then you will be able to correct him whom you love. And well does He say, *thou hypocrite!* For to bring up faults is the part of good and well-disposed people. When the bad do this, they are acting a part with which they have nothing to do, just like hypocrites, who hide behind a mask their actual selves and on the face of the mask impersonate what they are not. You will, therefore, take the term " hypocrites " to stand for pretenders. And there is, in fact, a class of pretenders, much to be guarded against and at the same time annoying who, while taking up in a spirit of hatred and spite accusations of every sort of wrongdoing, would also give themselves the appearance of counsellors. And we must be scrupulously careful to see to it that when the situation makes it incumbent on us to chide or rebuke someone, we first reflect whether the fault is one that we have never had or one from which we are now free. And if we have never had it, let us reflect that we are only human and might have had it. But if we have had it and no longer have it, let it be impressed upon the memory that here is a weakness shared by us, so that not hatred but pity will go out in advance of our chiding or upbraiding. Thus, whether it avails for the amendment of the person in whose behalf we do this, or for his undoing— the outcome, at any rate, is uncertain—we at least are sure of having a single-eyed purpose. But if on reflection we find ourselves involved in the same fault as he whom we are preparing to chide, let us not chide nor rebuke; but let us sorrow from our heart; let us invite him not to conform himself to us, but to join us in a common resolve.

65. For, considering also what the Apostle says: *I became to the Jews a Jew that I might gain the Jews; to them that*

are under the Law, as if under the Law—whereas myself am not under the Law—that I might gain them that were under the Law; to them that are without the Law, as if without the Law—whereas I am not without the Law of God but am in the Law of Christ—that I might gain them that are without the Law. To the weak I became weak, that I might gain the weak. I became all things to all men that I might gain all: [157] he certainly did not pretend to do this, as some would have us think, having in mind to support their detestable pretense by the authority of such an example; but he acted thus out of love, by which he regarded as his own the weakness of him whom he wished to help. This he also stated by way of preface, saying: *For whereas I am free as to all, I made myself a servant of all, that I might gain the more.*[158] And that you may realize that this comes about not by dissimulating, but through love which causes us to be sympathetic towards men as if we were they, he reminds us in another passage, saying: *You, brethren, have been called into liberty. Only make not liberty an occasion to the flesh; but by charity serve one another.*[159] And this cannot be done unless each one regards as his own the weakness of another, putting up with it in all calmness until he whose welfare he has at heart is freed from it.

66.   Rarely, therefore, and only under the compulsion of a great necessity are we to resort to upbraiding; and then only in such a way that in these instances, too, we make it our earnest endeavor to serve God, not ourselves. For here we have our final end and purpose: that we do nothing from a divided heart, taking from our eye the beam of jealousy or malice or pretense, so that we may see to take the mote from our brother's eye. Yes, we shall regard it with the eyes of the dove,[160] the eyes extolled in the Spouse of Christ, which God

has chosen for Himself *a glorious Church not having spot or wrinkle*,[161] that is, pure and without guile.

CHAPTER 20

The use of discrimination in offering the holy pearls of truth.

67. But because the word " guileless " can convey a false impression to some who are desirous to obey God's precepts, so that they may think it wrong to conceal the truth on occasion just as it is wrong to say at times what is false; and because in this way, by revealing things which they to whom they are revealed are not able to assimilate, they may do more harm than if they had completely and always concealed them, He very properly subjoins: *Give not that which is holy to dogs. Neither cast ye your pearls before swine, lest perhaps they trample them under their feet, and turning upon you, they tear you* (6). The Lord Himself, though He never lied, yet indicated that He was concealing certain truths, saying: *I have yet many things to say to you, but you cannot bear them now.*[162] And the Apostle Paul: *I could not speak to you as unto spiritual but as unto carnal, as unto little ones in Christ. I gave you milk to drink, not meat; for you were not able as yet. But neither indeed are you now able; for you are yet carnal.*[163]

68. Now, with reference to this precept that forbids us to give that which is holy to dogs and to cast our pearls before swine, we must make careful enquiry, as to what is meant by " holy," by " pearls," by " dogs," and by " swine." That is holy which it is impious to violate and impair. In any case,

already the attempt and will to commit such a crime involves guilt, even though of its nature the particular holy thing should remain inviolate and uncorruptible. As to the pearls, these are all the spiritual things that are to be highly treasured; and because they lie hidden away, they are drawn, as it were, out of the deep and found sheathed in allegory—in shells, one might say, that are opened. We may, therefore, conceive that one and the same thing can be called holy and a pearl; and holy from the fact that it should not be impaired, a pearl from the fact that it should not be despised. But one seeks to impair what he does not wish to be whole; he despises what he considers worthless and beneath him, so to speak; and so, whatever is despised is said to be trampled on. Wherefore, since dogs rush on an object to tear it to pieces, and what they tear to pieces they do not let whole—*Give not*, He said, *that which is holy to dogs*, because, even though it cannot be torn to pieces or impaired and remains whole and inviolate, yet we must consider what their intentions are who stand opposed to it like bitter enemies and, as much as lies in them, try to do away with the truth, were that possible. And regarding swine, though they do not, like dogs, attack by using their teeth, they befoul things by trampling about everywhere. Therefore, *cast not your pearls before swine, lest perhaps they trample them under their feet and turning upon you they tear you*. Therefore it is not out of keeping to interpret dogs as used for those who attack the truth, and swine for those who despise it.

69. But when He says: *turning upon you they tear you*, He does not say, "they tear the pearls themselves." In trampling on them, even when they turn to hear something further, they tear to pieces him who cast the pearls which they have already trampled on. For you will not easily find that

anything can be acceptable to him who has trampled on pearls, that is, who has despised divine things that have been discovered only with great labor. And as to him who teaches such people, how he is going to escape being torn to pieces by their fuming indignation, I fail to see. Moreover, both animals are unclean, the dog and the swine.

We must, therefore, beware of revealing anything to him who cannot receive it. It were better for him to seek what is closed than to carp at and disdain what has been thrown open to him. And there is no other reason for their non-acceptance of what is of manifest importance, save hatred and contempt; wherefore in the one case they have been called dogs, in the other, swine.

But all this uncleanness is conceived of a love of things temporal, that is, a love of this world, which we are ordered to renounce that we may be able to be clean. One, therefore, who desires to have a clean and guileless heart ought not to feel guilty if he conceals anything from him who cannot receive it. Nor must the impression be taken from this that lying is a licit thing; for it does not follow that in concealing the truth falsehood is uttered. The first thing to do, then, is to remove the hindrances which bring about his failure to be receptive. For certainly if it is his untidy condition that renders him unreceptive, he must be made clean either by word or by deed as far as that is possible for us.

70. Again, as to the fact that Our Lord is found to have said certain things which many who were present did not receive because of their resistance or contempt, it is not to be thought that He had given what is holy to dogs or had cast pearls before swine. He did not give such things to those who could not receive them, but to those who could and were present with the others. He could not neglect them just

because others were unclean. And while hecklers were putting questions to Him and He answered them in a manner that left them no ground for rejoinder, and though they preferred to be sapped by their own poisons than to appease their hunger by His food, yet others who were receptive and as a result of the opportunity created by such persons heard a great deal which they could turn to their advantage. I have mentioned this so that no one when he is unable to give satisfaction to a questioner, may imagine himself excused by the formula that he does not care to give holy things to dogs or cast pearls before swine. To be sure, if a person knows the answer, he ought to give it, if but for the sake of others who lose hope if they are led to believe that the question proposed cannot be answered; and here there is reference to matters of a practical nature and that have to do with the schooling on one's salvation. There are, of course, many questions idlers can propose, serving no purpose, mere chatter, and often enough causing harm; but something must be said in such cases, and this precisely needs to be made crystal-clear—why such questions should not be asked.

In practical matters, therefore, we must sometimes answer questions directly as put; as did the Lord when the Sadducees had questioned him about the woman who had had seven husbands and whose wife she was going to be in the resurrection. His answer was that *in the resurrection they would neither marry nor be married, but would be as the angels in heaven.*[164] There are occasions, too, when the questioner should be asked in turn, answering which he will answer his own question; and if then he refuses to reply, those present will not deem it unfair if he himself does not receive an answer to his question. For those, too, who asked Him— meaning to embarrass Him—whether it was their duty to pay the tax, were asked another question, namely, whose was the image on the coin which they showed Him; and because they replied to the question asked of them, that is to say, that the coin bore Caesar's image, in a way they answered the very question they had put to the Lord; and so it was from their answer He drew the conclusion: *Render, therefore, to Caesar the things that are Caesar's; and to God the things that are God's.*[165] When, however, the chief priests and elders of the people questioned Him on what authority He was doing those things, He questioned them about the baptism of John; and when they were unwilling to give an answer because they saw their answer would tell against them, and regarding John they dared not say anything derogatory in the presence of the people, He said: *Neither do I tell you by what authority I do these things;*[166] and the bystanders thought that perfectly fair. For they stated that they did not know what they knew full well, simply because they were unwilling to speak out. And it was indeed but right that they who wanted an answer to their question should themselves first do what they were asking to be done to them; and had they done so, they would assuredly have answered their own question. For it was they who had sent to John enquiring of him who he was;[167] or rather, they themselves, the priests and levites, had been sent, supposing that he was the Christ. He said that he was not; and he gave witness concerning the Lord. Had they wished to make admission of this witnessing, they would have demonstrated to themselves by what authority Christ was doing those things. But they asked about this as if they did not know, in order to find an opening for slander.

CHAPTER 21

Ask, seek, knock.

71. When, therefore, the precept had been given not to give that which is holy to dogs nor cast pearls before swine, someone in the audience, conscious of his own ignorance and weakness and hearing that he was ordered not to give what he knew he had not yet himself received, might have objected and said: "What is this holy thing you forbid me to give to dogs and what are these pearls you forbid me to cast before swine? I do not see that I have such things as yet." Most opportunely He added, saying: *Ask, and it shall be given you; seek, and you shall find; knock, and it shall be opened to you. For every one that asketh, receiveth; and he that seeketh, findeth; and to him that knocketh, it shall be opened* (7 f.). The asking has to do with obtaining that health and strength of soul which will enable us to fulfill the commandments enjoined on us; the seeking, with finding the truth. For since the blessed life is perfected by action and knowledge, action stands in need of a reserve of strength, and contemplation looks to the clarification of things. Of these, therefore, the first is to be asked for, the second, sought for; so that the one may be given, the other, found. However, in this life knowledge marks the way rather than the possession itself; but once a person finds the true way he will arrive at possession itself, which, again, is thrown open to him who knocks.[168]

72. In order, therefore, to have a clear picture of these three things—asking, seeking, knocking [169]—let us take the example of someone unable to walk because his feet will not

support him. First, then, he must be restored to health and made strong so he can walk; and to this pertains what He said: *Ask.* But what is the benefit of being able to walk, or even to run, if he wanders on roundabout roads? Consequently the second thing is to find the road that leads to his objective. And if then, on keeping to that road and coming to the place where he wishes to remain, he finds it closed, he has gained nothing by his ability to walk or by his actual walking and arriving, unless it be opened to him; to this, therefore, pertains what was said: *Knock.*

73. And He who does not fail His promises has given and continues to give great hope; for He said: *every one that asketh, receiveth; and he that seeketh, findeth; and to him that knocketh, it shall be opened.* Therefore, what we need is perseverance, that we may receive what we ask for and find what we seek and have opened to us when we knock. As He cited the birds of the air and the lilies of the field that we might not despair of the presence of food and raiment and that thus our hope might rise from the lesser to the greater; so here again: *Or what man will there be among you, of whom if his son shall ask bread, will he reach him a stone? Or if he shall ask him a fish, will he reach him a serpent? If you then being evil, know how to give good gifts to your children, how much more will your Father who is in heaven give good things to them that ask Him* (9-11)? How do the evil give good things? Well, He designated as evil those who are still lovers of this world and sinners. As to the good things which they give, they are to be called good according to their meaning because they consider them good; though also in the natural order such things are good, but temporal and belonging to this present impotent life of ours; and if any evil person gives them, he gives not of his own,

for *the earth is the Lord's and the fullness thereof, who made heaven and earth, the sea and all things in them.*[170] How great, then, should be our confidence that God will give us good things when we ask them, and that we cannot be deceived so as to ask Him for one thing and to receive another—realizing as we do that even we, evil though we be, know how to give what is asked of us! For we do not deceive our children; and whatever good things we give, we give not from our own, but from what is His.

CHAPTER 22

The Golden Rule.

74. Further, a certain strength and ability to walk in the way of wisdom lies in good conduct persevered in until the heart's cleansing and its singleness are achieved, about which subject He has been speaking for long and which He concludes thus: *All good things, therefore, whatsoever you would that men should do to you, do you also to them. For this is the Law and the Prophets* (12). In the Greek versions we find this: *All things, therefore, whatsoever you would that men should do to you, do you also to them.* By the Latins " good " was added to clarify the meaning, I believe.[171] For the thought suggested itself that if someone wished something wicked done to him and for this purpose would allege this text; for example, if a person wished to be challenged to drink immoderately and to swill himself in his cups and first practiced this upon the person by whom he wished it to be performed upon himself: it would then be ridiculous for such a person to suppose that he had lived up to this prescription. Therefore, inasmuch as this caused some apprehension,

I suppose one word was added to clarify the matter; so that in the statement: *All things, therefore, whatsoever you would that men should do to you,* there was inserted the word " good." Now, if this is lacking in the Greek copies, they also ought to be amended; but who would venture to do this? It is to be understood, therefore, that the statement is complete and quite perfect even without the addition of this word. For the expression used, " whatsoever you would," should not be taken as spoken in a broad, general sense, but with a restricted application: that is to say, the will is present only in the good; in evil and wicked actions cupidity is the word, not will. Not that Scripture always speaks in a restricted sense; but where it must, it so restricts a word's meaning that it suffers no other interpretation of it.

75. Moreover, apparently this precept pertains to the love of neighbor and not also to the love of God, since in another place He says that there are two precepts on which *dependeth the whole Law and the Prophets.*[172] For if He had said: " All things whatsoever you would should be done to you, this do you also," in this one sentence He would have embraced both these precepts. For then it would be suggested at once that everyone wished himself to be loved both by God and by man; and thus, when this was enjoined on him, that what he wished done to himself he should himself do, there certainly was given the precept that he should love God and man. However, since this was said with express reference to men: *All things, therefore, whatsoever you would that men should do to you, do you also to them,* no other injunction seems laid down than: *Thou shalt love thy neighbor as thyself.*[173] But we must carefully note what He added here: *for this is the Law and the Prophets.* On the other hand, He not merely said: *On these two commandments dependeth the*

Law and the Prophets; but He also made an addition: "the *whole* Law and the Prophets," meaning the same as all prophecy.[174] But by not making the same addition here, He left room for the other precept which pertains to the love of God. Here, moreover, since He is continuing close upon precepts enjoining singleness of heart, and because this is to be feared that a person have duplicity in his heart towards those from whom the heart can be hid, that is, towards men, therefore that very thing had to be prescribed. For there is scarcely anyone who wishes a person to treat him with a double-hearted intention. But this is an impossibility, that is to say, for man to bestow anything upon another with a single-hearted intention unless he bestows it without expecting any temporal advantage from him, and does it with the motivation concerning which we have gone into sufficient detail above when we were speaking of the single eye.

76. Therefore, once the eye has been cleansed and made single, it will be fit and capable of beholding and contemplating its own interior light. For that eye is the eye of the heart. And an eye such as this is the possession of him who, in order that his works may be truly good, does not seek the pleasure of his fellow men as the purpose of his good works; and even if it turns out that he pleases them, he relates this to their welfare and God's glory instead of turning it to empty boasting. Nor does he do any good conducive to his neighbor's welfare with the motive of gaining thereby what is needed to come through this life; nor is he so rash as to pass condemnatory judgment on a man's attitude and intention in a matter where it is not apparent with what attitude and intention a thing has been done. Again, whatever service he renders to another he renders it with the intention he would like manifested towards himself, that is, of not ex-

pecting any temporal favor from him. Here is your heart single and pure—the heart in which God is sought. *Blessed, therefore, are the clean of heart for they shall see God.*

CHAPTER 23

The strait way and the narrow gate.

77. But because such is the case with few, He now begins to speak of searching out and coming into the possession of wisdom which is *the tree of life;* [175] and indeed, in the search of this wisdom and its possession, that is, its contemplation, the eye we have been speaking about has been introduced to all that goes before, so that now the strait road and the narrow gate are visible. Respecting, therefore, what He proceeds to say: *Enter ye in at the narrow gate; for wide is the gate and broad is the way that leadeth to destruction; and many there are who go in thereat. How narrow is the gate and strait the way that leadeth to life; and few there are who find it* (13 f.)! He does not say this because the yoke of the Lord is galling or His burden heavy, but because few wish their labors to be ended, giving scant trust to Him who cries: *Come to me, all you that labor . . . and I will refresh you. Take up my yoke and learn of me, because I am meek and humble of heart. . . . For my yoke is smooth and my burden light;* [176] and hence it was that this sermon took its beginning—from the lowly and meek of heart. And this smooth yoke and light burden many spurn, few submit to; and so it comes about that the way which leads to life is strait and the gate by which it is entered is narrow.

CHAPTER 24

Beware of false prophets.

78. Here, then, we are to be particularly on our guard against those who promise wisdom and knowledge of the truth which they do not possess; such, for example, are heretics, who very often advance their small following as a recommendation of themselves.[177] And therefore, when He had said there are few who find the narrow gate and the strait way, to keep such people from making false pretensions by alleging their small numbers, He immediately added: *Beware of false prophets who come to you in the clothing of sheep, but inwardly they are ravening wolves* (15). But these do not deceive the single-visioned eye which knows how to recognize a tree by its fruits. For He says: *By their fruits you shall know them.* He then adds these comparisons: *Do men gather grapes of thorns, or figs of thistles? Even so every good tree bringeth forth good fruit and the evil tree bringeth forth evil fruit. A good tree cannot bring forth evil fruit, neither can an evil tree bring forth good fruit. Indeed, every tree that bringeth not forth good fruit shall be cut down and shall be cast into the fire. Wherefore by their fruits you shall know them* (16-20).

79. With respect to this passage, we must especially shun the error of those who from these same two trees draw the notion that there are two natures, one of which is God's, but the other, neither God's nor from God. This error has already been subjected to thorough treatment in other books, and if that is still not enough, the discussion will continue;[178]

but in the present instance we have merely to point out that the two trees mentioned do not help them. First, because it is so clear that He is speaking about men that whoever reads what goes before and what follows, will be astonished at their blindness. Next, they note the statement: *A good tree cannot bring forth evil fruit, neither can an evil tree bring forth good fruit*; and so they think that it cannot happen that an evil soul should undergo a change for the better, or a good soul change for the worse—as if it had been said: " A good tree cannot become evil nor an evil tree become good." What was actually said is: *A good tree cannot bring forth evil fruit, neither can an evil tree bring forth good fruit*. The tree, to be sure, is the soul itself, that is, man himself, and the fruits are man's works. An evil person, therefore, cannot do good works nor a good person evil works. Hence, if an evil person wishes to do good works, let him first become good. This is what the Lord Himself states more clearly in another place: *Either make the tree good . . . , or make the tree evil.*[179] And if by these two trees He had meant to represent the two natures of the people referred to, He would never have said, " make." For what man is there that can make a nature? Then, too, in the very context where He had made mention of these two trees, He subjoined: *Hypocrites, how can you speak good things whereas you are evil?* [180] As long, therefore, as a person is evil he cannot bring forth good fruits; for if he brings forth good fruits, he will no longer be evil. In the same way in a very true sense it could have been said, snow cannot be warm; for when it begins to be warm, we no longer call it snow, but water. Thus it can happen that what was snow no longer is such; but it cannot happen that snow should be warm. So it can come about that one who was bad is no longer bad; but it cannot come about that a bad person should do good. Granted, moreover, that he sometimes proves helpful: but this is not of his doing, but part of the economy of Divine Providence, as was said of the Pharisees: *What they say, do; but what they do, do ye not.*[181] The fact that they spoke things that were for the good and the people profited from hearing them and that thus they proved helpful, was not of their doing; for, He said, *they sit on the chair of Moses.*[182] When, therefore, by the arrangement of Divine Providence they were proclaiming the law of God, it was possible for them to advance their hearers while not doing the same to themselves. Of such it is stated in another place through the Prophet: *You have sown wheat and you are reaping thorns* [183]—because they prescribe what is good and do what is evil. Those who heard them and did what they said were not therefore gathering grapes of thorns, but, reaching through the thorns, they picked grapes from the vine: just as when a man reaches his hand through a hedge or otherwise picks a grape from a vine entangled in a hedge, that would not be the fruit of the thorns, but of the vine.

80. The question is certainly most justified as to what fruits He wishes us to look for that by them we can recognize the tree. For many see among the fruits certain things which are proper to the sheep's clothing and in this way are deceived by the wolves. Such are, for example, fasting, prayers, almsdeeds—all things which if it were not possible for hypocrites to perform also, He would not have said earlier: *Take heed that you do not your justice before men, to be seen by them.*[184] After prefixing this statement, He follows with these three things—alms, prayer, fasting. Many there are who give much to the poor not from compassion, but to be well-thought-of. Again, many pray, or rather appear to pray, not

with their heart set on God, but set on attracting men's pleasure. And many, too, fast and display an astounding self-restraint before those who deem this difficult and worthy of commendation; and catch them by frauds of this kind, the while they parade one thing to beguile them and put forth another to seduce or slay persons who cannot see under that sheep's clothing the wolves that they are. These, therefore, are not the fruits whereby He informs us that the tree is recognized. It is these same things done with an upright disposition in sincerity that are the real clothing of sheep; when done with an evil disposition with insincerity, they are nothing else than covering for wolves. But the sheep must not for this reason hate their own clothing because wolves often use it to conceal themselves.

81. Now, then, as to what the fruits are by the finding of which we may recognize a bad tree, the Apostle says: *Now the works of the flesh are manifest: which are fornication, uncleanness, luxuries, idolatries, witchcrafts, enmities, contentions, emulations, wraths, dissensions, heresies, sects, envies, drunkenness, revellings and such like. Of the which I foretell you, as I have foretold you, that they who do such things shall not possess the kingdom of God.*[185] And what the fruits are by which we can recognize a good tree, the same goes on to say: *But the fruit of the Spirit is charity, joy, peace, longanimity, benignity, goodness, faith, mildness, continency.*[186] It is well to note that " joy " in this passage is used in a restricted sense: evil men are, properly speaking, not said to rejoice but to revel; [187] just as we have said above that " will," which evil people do not have, is used in a restricted sense where it is said: *All things whatsoever you would that men should do to you, do you also to them.* From this strict acceptation of the word whereby " joy " is spoken

of as being only in the good, the Prophet also speaks, saying: *There is no joy for the wicked, saith the Lord.*[188] So also " faith " is mentioned, not indeed any version of it, but true faith; and the other things which are here listed have certain reflections of their own in evil men and deceivers, so that they prove quite delusive unless one's eye is clear and single-visioned enough to recognize them for what they are. And so the arrangement was best whereby the cleansing of the eye was taken first and then the things that were to be guarded against.

CHAPTER 25

Warnings: Speech is not a sure indicator of the interior man; nor are his deeds. Once again: The finding of the way of wisdom requires an eye that is clear and single-visioned. Conclusion: Hearing Christ's precepts, it is for us to carry them out.

82. But because, however clear an eye one may have, that is, however guileless and sincere of heart he may be, he yet cannot look into the heart of another; whatever fails to reveal itself through the words or deeds is made evident through temptations. Now, temptation is twofold: it is present either in the hope of gaining some temporal advantage or in the fear of losing it. And we must be incessantly on our guard, as we bend our efforts towards the wisdom that can be found only in Christ—*in whom are hid all the treasures of wisdom and knowledge* [189]—I repeat, we must be on our guard, lest under the very name of Christ we be deceived by

heretics or anyone else with twisted ideas and by lovers of this world. For to this end He follows with a warning, saying: *Not everyone that saith to me, "Lord, Lord," shall enter into the kingdom of heaven but he that doth the will of my Father who is in heaven, he shall enter into the kingdom of heaven* (21). We are not to think that if one merely addresses our Lord with "Lord, Lord," this has anything to do with those fruits and we consequently put him down as a good tree. But the fruits consist in this—to do the will of the Father who is in heaven; and of how this is to be done He deigned to give Himself as an example.

83. But the question may cause some concern—and rightly: what agreement with this statement is there in that of the Apostle where he says: *No man speaking by the Spirit of God saith "Anathema to Jesus." And no man can say "The Lord Jesus" but by the Holy Ghost?* [190] For plainly we cannot say that some who have the Holy Spirit will not enter the kingdom of heaven if they persevere unto the end; nor can we say that those who say "*Lord, Lord,*" and yet do not enter the kingdom, have the Holy Spirit. How, then, does no one say "*The Lord Jesus*" but by the *Holy Ghost*, save that the Apostle used the word "say" in a restricted sense, to signify the will and understanding of the speaker? The Lord, however, used the word in a general sense when He said: *Not everyone that saith to me, "Lord, Lord," shall enter into the kingdom of heaven.* For he, too, who neither wishes nor understands what he says, seems to say it; but, strictly speaking, only he actually says it who puts his mind and heart into the words he uses. As was said a moment ago about the word "joy" among the fruits of the Spirit: that it was used in a strict sense; not in the sense in which the same Apostle uses it elsewhere: *Rejoiceth not in*

iniquity.[191] As if anyone could rejoice over iniquity! Plainly, in such case we have the elation of a mind riotously exultant —not joy; for this is something that the good alone have. So, then, also those appear to be saying what they neither advert to in their mind nor make a matter of their will as they utter it—merely making sounds with their voice; and it was with this manner in view that the Lord said: *Not everyone that saith to me, "Lord, Lord," shall enter into the kingdom of heaven.* But they do truly and properly " say " it who do not permit their use of speech to be at odds with what is in their will and mind; and it is in this sense that the Apostle said: *No one can say "The Lord Jesus" but by the Holy Ghost.*

84. And, moreover, this eminently belongs here: that as we strive after the contemplation of the truth, we should not only not be deceived by Christ's name in the mouth of those who have His name but do not have His works, but also not by certain deeds and even miracles. When the Lord performed these because of unbelievers, He warned us not to be deceived by such things into believing that in every instance there is an invisible wisdom where we see a visible miracle. Hence He continues and says: *Many will say to me in that day: "Lord, Lord, have we not prophesied in Thy name and cast out devils in Thy name and done many miracles in Thy name?" And then will I say unto them: "I never knew you. Depart from me, you that work iniquity"* (22 f.). Hence He will recognize no one save him who works goodness. For He told even His disciples not to rejoice over such things, that is, that demons were subject unto them; *But rejoice in this,* He said, *that your names are written in heaven:*[192] in that city of Jerusalem, I take it, which is in heaven, where only the just and holy will reign. *Know you*

not, says the Apostle, *that the unjust shall not possess the kingdom of God?* [193]

85. But perhaps someone may say that it is impossible for wicked persons to perform such visible miracles, and would rather believe such people to be lying should they say: *We have prophesied in Thy name and cast out devils in Thy name and done many miracles in Thy name.* Well, let him read what great things the magicians of Egypt did in their resistance to Moses, the servant of God.[194] Or, if he will not read this because they did not do them in the name of Christ, let him read what the Lord Himself says about false prophets, speaking thus: *Then if any man say to you: " Lo, here is Christ, or there "—do not believe him. For there shall arise false Christs and false prophets and shall show great signs and wonders, insomuch as to deceive . . . even the elect. Behold, I have told it to you beforehand.*[195]

86. What need, therefore, is there that the eye be clear and single-visioned for the finding of the way to wisdom, whose voice so great a host of errors and deceptions of wicked and perverse men tries to drown out, and the avoidance of all of which constitutes the surest peace and the imperturbable security of wisdom! It is much to be feared that in his zeal to answer back and argue one may not see what only a few can see, that the clamor of the opposition is really trifling, unless it be that the person himself is in disagreement with himself. To this applies, too, what the Apostle says: *But the servant of the Lord must not wrangle, but be mild towards all men, apt to teach, patient, with modesty admonishing them who think differently—if peradventure God may give them repentance to know the truth.*[196] *Blessed, therefore, are the peacemakers, for they shall be called the children of God.*

87. For this reason, too, special attention is due to the conclusion of this whole sermon [197]—how terrifyingly it is driven home: *Every one, therefore, that heareth these my words and doth them, is like to a wise man that built his house upon a rock* (24). Now, no one makes positive of what he hears and perceives save by action. And if Christ is the rock—as many a passage in Scripture proclaims [198]—he builds on Christ who carries out what he hears from Him. *The rain fell, the floods came, the winds blew and they beat upon that house; and it fell not, for it was founded on a rock* (25). He, therefore, fears no gloomy superstitions—for what other meaning is conveyed by " rain " when it is placed in the signification of some evil?—or the speculations of men, whom I here think likened to the winds; or the floodwater of this life with its carnal concupiscences inundating, as it were, the earth. If a man is seduced by the success held out by these three, he is broken by the reverses that follow in their wake. But he has no fear of them who has built his house upon a rock, that is, who not only hears the Lord's precepts, but also carries them out. It is he who hears them but does not carry them out that is in immediate danger of all three. He simply has no secure foundation; but by hearing and not acting accordingly he is building ruin. For He says next: *And every one that heareth these my words and doth them not, shall be like a foolish man that buildeth his house upon the sand: the rain fell, the floods came, the winds blew and they beat upon that house; and it fell, and great was the fall thereof* (26 f.).

And it came to pass when Jesus had fully ended these words, the people were in admiration at His doctrine. For He was teaching them as one having power and not as their Scribes (28 f.). This is what I said before had been signified in the Psalms by the Prophet when he said: *I will deal confidently in his regard. The words of the Lord are pure words, as silver tried by the fire, purged from the earth, refined seven times.*[199]

Here it was this number seven which suggested to me that these precepts also hark back to those seven maxims which He put at the head of this sermon when He spoke the Beatitudes, and to those seven operations of the Holy Spirit of which the Prophet Isaias makes mention.[200] But whether the order here given should be observed or some other, we must do what we have heard from the Lord if we wish to build upon a rock.

NOTES

INTRODUCTION

[1] The great amount of literature dealing with this sermon can be found in the commentaries to the New Testament. For a more recent analysis, see T. Soiron, *Die Bergpredigt Jesu. Formgeschichtliche, exegetische und theologische Erklärung* (Freiburg i. Br. 1941). Cf. also R. Stoll, "The Sermon on the Mount," *Am. Eccles. Rev.* 104 (1941) 193-209, 301-318, 395-411.

[2] Cf. H. Vogels, "Synoptische Studien zur Bergpredigt," *Bonner Zeitschr. f. Theol. u. Seelsorge* 1 (1924) 123-36.

[3] Others think that the Sermon on the Mount was meant for the Apostles and the missionary period only. Cf. K. Bornhäuser, *Die Bergpredigt. Versuch einer zeitgenössischen Auslegung* (2nd ed., Gütersloh 1927); A. Steinmann, *Die Bergpredigt. Kritische Bemerkungen zu einer neuen Auslegung* (Braunsberg 1925).

[4] Cf. J. Weiss, *Die Predigt vom Reiche Gottes* (Göttingen 1892); A. Schweitzer, *Kulturphilosophie II: Kultur und Ethik* (Zürich 1923).

[5] Cf. C. Stange, "Zur Ethik der Bergpredigt," *Zeitschr. f. syst. Theol.* 2 (1924) 37-74; G. Kittel, "Die Bergpredigt und die Ethik des Judentums," *ibid.* 3 (1925) 555-94; A. Runestam, "Das ethische Problem der Bergpredigt," *ibid.* 4 (1926) 555-72.

[6] Cf. O. Baumgarten, *Bergpredigt und Kultur der Gegenwart* (Tübingen 1921); R. Hermann, *Die Bergpredigt und die Religiös-Sozialen* (Leipzig 1922); M. Dibelius, *The Sermon on the Mount* (New York 1940); H. Windisch, *Der Sinn der Bergpredigt* (2nd ed., Leipzig 1937).

[7] Cf. J. Ackermann, *Tolstoi und das Neue Testament* (Diss. Leipzig 1927).

[8] Cf. H. Windisch, "Friedensbringer-Gottessöhne. Eine religionsgeschichtliche Interpretation der 7. Seligpreisung," *Zeitschr. f. Neutest. Wiss.* 24 (1925) 240-60.

[9] See Augustine, *Serm.* 179. 4-6; *Serm.* 103. 4, 5; *Serm.* 104. Cf. C. Butler, *Western Mysticism* (2nd ed., London 1927) 227-42.

[10] *De Trin.* 12. 14. 21-23; 15. 25.

[11] *Adv. haer.* 3. 17. 1; 4. 13. 2; 16. 3.

[12] *In 2 Cor.* 3. 3-6; *In Rom.* 8. 2; *In Gal.* 5. 23.

[13] *De spir. et litt.* 36.

[14] *Summa theol.* 1. 2, 106-8.

[15] Cf. D. Bassi, " Le beatitudine nella struttura de De sermone Dei in monte e nelle altre opere di S. Agostino," *Misc. Agost.* 2 (Rome 1931) 915-31. See also G. Morin, " Sermon inédit de S. Augustin sur les huit béatitudes," *Rev. Bén.* 34 (1922) 1-13.

[16] Cf. O. Tescari, *L'orazione del Signore interpretata da S. Agostino* (Turin 1939).

[17] Cf. F. Ventro, *Il sermone sulla montagna e le parabole commentate per le scuole medie* (Catania 1926).

[18] See A. Gardeil, " Béatitudes évangéliques," *Dict. de théol. cath.* 12 (1923) 515-7; M. D. Roland-Gosselin, " Le sermon sur la montagne et la théologie thomiste," *Rev. des scienc. philosoph. et théol.* 17 (1928) 201-234.

[19] This volume also provides a reprint of the Latin text in the recension of St. Maur. Unfortunately, misprints are numerous, some of which alter the meaning of the original text.

BOOK ONE

[1] Matt. 7. 24-27. The Vulgate has *assimilabitur*, 'shall be likened,' and *similis erit*, 'shall be like,' for *similabo*, 'I shall liken' (near the end of the treatise, 2. 25. 87, A. has *similis est* and *similis erit*). There are other differences: for the Vulgate *irruerunt*, 'beat upon,' St. Augustine has the synonym *offenderunt*; and he does not use *et* to join *descendit pluvia, venerunt flumina, flaverunt venti*. In partial fulfillment of the commission given him by Pope Damasus to provide a revision of the Latin Bible, St. Jerome in 383 published the Gospels. St. Augustine followed this part of the Vulgate from the year 400 onward. He wrote the present treatise in approximately the year 394—at a time, therefore, when he had not yet adopted St. Jerome's version. For a composite picture of the Old Latin Gospel texts followed by St. Augustine at this time, see the scholarly study of C. H. Milne: *A Reconstruction of the Old Latin Text or Texts of the Gospels Used by Saint Augustine* (Cambridge 1926).

[2] Ps. 35. 7.

[3] Eccle. 1. 14, according to the Old Latin versions of the Septuagint.

[4] Ps. 148. 8.

[5] 1 Cor. 8. 1.

[6] Eccli. 1. 16.

[7] *Ibid.* 10. 15.

[8] The Vulgate does not have *haereditate*, 'by inheritance.' This addition by Augustine becomes clear from the version used by St. Cyprian (*Test.* 3. 5): quoniam ipsi *haereditabunt* terram: 'for they shall inherit the land'; this reflects the original Greek κληρονομήσουσιν, the literal sense of which is 'shall inherit' but which commonly also means 'shall possess.' Moreover, the words of this second Beatitude are based on Ps. 36. 11: 'But the meek shall inherit (*haereditabunt*, κληρονομήσουσιν) the earth.'

[9] Ps. 141. 6.

[10] Cf. Rom. 12. 21.

[11] John 4. 34. The Vulgate reads 'of Him that sent me' for 'my Father.'

[12] *Ibid.* 4. 14.

[13] Wisd. 1. 1.

[14] Cf. Luke 2. 14.

[15] For the term, cf. John 12. 31; 14. 30; 16. 11. Ignatius of Antioch used the term very frequently: *Ephes.* 17. 1; *Magn.* 1; *Trall.* 4; *Rom.* 7; *Philad.* 6.

[16] *Rom.* 8. 35.

[17] Isa. 11. 2 f.: 'And the spirit of the Lord shall rest upon him; the spirit of *wisdom* and of *understanding*, the spirit of *counsel* and of *fortitude*, the spirit of *knowledge* and of *godliness*; and He shall be filled with the spirit of *the fear of the Lord.*' For the inversion in the following of the order of the Gifts of the Holy Spirit as given here by Isaias; see also *Serm.* 348. 2; also the Introduction 7; below, 203 f. nn. 92 and 93. Regarding the significance for theology of this association of the Gifts of the Holy Spirit with the Beatitudes, read also F. Cayré, " Contemplation et raison d'après Saint Augustin," *Mélanges Augustiniens* (= *Rev. de Phil.* 30, nouvelle sér. 1, Paris 1931) 346.

[18] Eccli. 1. 16.

[19] Rom. 11. 20.

[20] 1 Cor. 2. 9; cf. Isa. 64. 4.

[21] St. Augustine later corrected himself here (*Retract.* 1. 19. 1): No matter how faithfully the human soul withholds its assent from temptation, never in this life is there a time when man is utterly free from evil surgings, when with the *lex mentis* there is not also present a *lex in membris* to fight back against it.

[22] Here again Augustine later thought that he should caution his reader (*Retract.* 1. 19. 2). He states that he did not imply that the Apostles in their lives were free from unruly passions. The perfection enjoyed by them was, after all, a limited one, one not equal to the one we hope to have in the afterlife *pace plenissima*.

[23] That is, the octave of Easter, on which feast the ancient Church held the solemn administration of baptism. Regarding the Easter Octave, cf. especially the unique account—written perhaps some few years previous to St. Augustine's present treatise—by the pilgrim nun Aetheria on her visit in Jerusalem and the Holy Land: *Peregrinatio ad loca sancta*, chapters 39 and 40. She speaks of the Easter solemnity at Jerusalem as extending *per octo dies*, ' over eight days '; and significantly adds, ' as is the case everywhere else.' Regarding Easter, the Easter Octave, and the early Easter controversies, read K. A. H. Kellner, *Heortology: A History of the Christian Festivals from their Origin to the Present Day* (trans. from the 2nd German ed. by ' a priest of the Diocese of Westminster,' London 1908) 37 ff.

[23a] The name Pentecost (Fiftieth Day) is found already in the Old

Testament: 2 Mac. 12. 32. It was a 'festival of (seven) weeks'
(cf. Deut. 16. 10) after Easter—the fiftieth day. Cf. A. Steinmann,
Die Apostelgeschichte (4th ed., Bonn 1934) 28. For a more elaborate
discussion of the number " 7 "—*septenarius numerus*—in the operation of the Holy Spirit on Pentecost, cf. Augustine, *Serm.* 8. 11. 13.

[24] Ps. 44. 14.

[25] Rom. 5. 3-5.

[26] St. Cyprian had the same conviction; cf. *De Eccl. unit.* 14:
' Tales enim si occisi in confessione nominis fuerint, macula ista nec
sanguine abluitur: inexpiabilis et gravis culpa discordiae nec passione
purgatur. *Esse martyr non potest qui in Ecclesia non est.*' Cf. *ibid.*
19; *Ep.* 60. 4.

[27] Rom. 1. 17; cf. Hab. 2. 4.

[28] Rom. 13. 10. Heretics have no charity: a refrain found again
and again in Augustine's works against the Donatists; cf. especially
De bapt. c. Don. 1. 13. 21 ff. Because of their hatred for their
Christian brethren they, moreover, make themselves guilty of homi-
cide, as Scripture testifies (1 John 3. 15): 'Whosoever hateth his
brother is a murderer'; cf. *C. litt. Petil.* 2. 20. 46.

[29] Col. 1. 24.

[30] John 8. 48.

[31] *Ibid.* 7. 12. The Vulgate has ' good man ' for ' prophet.'

[32] Gen. 3. 19.

[33] Phil. 3. 20.

[34] 1 Cor. 15. 53.

[35] 2 Cor. 5. 10.

[36] Matt. 7. 2.

[37] John 3. 34. In *Retract.* 1. 19. 3, St. Augustine states that at the
time he wrote his treatise on the Sermon on the Mount he did not
yet grasp that to Christ alone *God doth not give the Spirit by
measure.* If this were not so, he adds, Eliseus would not have asked
for double the spirit of Elias (cf. 4 Kings 2. 9).

[38] 1 Cor. 3. 26 f.

[39] Gal. 1. 10.

[40] Ps. 52. 6.

[41] *Ibid.* The Vulgate reads the entire verse thus: 'For God hath
scattered the bones of them that please men: they have been
confounded, because God hath despised them.'

[42] Gal. 5. 26.

[43] *Ibid.* 6. 4.

[44] Matt. 9. 8.

[45] Gal. 1. 23 f.

[46] Once again the author, as he reviewed this work of his earlier years, decided that he should have written with soberer pen. He states (*Retract.* 1. 19. 3) that the perfection here spoken of must be limited to provide for the bitter fact: that no man retaining the faculty of a free will actually lives on earth without sin. He adds that the plea *forgive us our debts as we also forgive our debtors* is one 'which the Church pronounces to the end.'

[47] Our Lord spoke of the *jot*, the smallest letter in the Hebrew-Aramaic alphabet, to which corresponds the *iota* of the New Testament. The tittle (*apex*, κεραία) was a dot or small sign used in writing (note the tittle—dot—over the modern 'i' or 'j,' the equivalents of *jot* or *iota*).

[48] The author states in *Retract.* 1. 19. 4, that in his later discussions he has given a much better and more correct interpretation of this passage (cf. e. g., *De fide et op.* 36. 48; *In Ioan. Ev. tract.* 122. 9; *De civ. Dei* 20. 9). The justice of those abounds more, Augustine explains, who not only preach what is good, but also perform it themselves; this the Scribes and Pharisees did not do, as the Lord said (Matt. 23. 3): 'They say, and do not.'

[49] Augustine later dropped the phrase *sine causa*, 'without cause,' when he found that there was no justification for it in the Greek codices; cf. *Retract.* 1. 19. 4. St. Cyprian also read *sine causa* (cf. *Test.* 3. 8) as did St. John Chrysostom among the Greeks (cf. *In Matt. hom.* 16. 7—*sine causa* = εἰκῇ).

[49a] 'Ragged,' 'ragged person,' 'ragamuffin.'

[50] Augustine's informant appears to have spoken truthfully; though many scholars have studied the word ῥακά (for the literature, cf. W. Bauer, *Griechisch-deutsches Wörterbuch zu den Schriften des Neuen Testaments und der übrigen urchristlichen Literatur* [3rd ed., Berlin 1937] *s. v.*), they do not appear to agree on its derivation and precise meaning except to find in it an expression of extreme contempt. St. John Chrysostom (*In Matt. hom.* 16. 7) found only slight contempt expressed by the word. F. Zorell, *Lexicon Graecum Novi Testamenti* (2nd ed., Paris 1931) *s. v.*, rightly asks: 'Verum quadratne haec opinio in verba Christi tam severa?'

[51] Referring to Matt. 5. 21: "You have heard that it was said to them of old: 'Thou shalt not kill'; and whosoever shall kill shall be in danger of the judgment." The 'other' case refers to the following verse: "But I say to you that whosoever is angry with his brother, shall be in danger of the judgment."

⁵²Gal. 3. 1.
⁵³For example, Gal. 1. 11, and at least a half-dozen times more.
⁵⁴Eph. 4. 26.
⁵⁵1 Cor. 3. 17.
⁵⁶Eph. 3. 17.
⁵⁷Here the repetition and application of the first Beatitude is significant. In the last lines of our treatise Augustine very briefly states that also in his discussion of the new or 'greater' precepts as proclaimed in the Sermon on the Mount he was conscious of a relationship between these and the Beatitudes and the Gifts of the Holy Spirit. Quoting the Psalmist (11. 7), *The words of the Lord are pure words, as silver tried by the fire, purged from the earth, refined seven times,* he states:

> Here it was this number seven which suggested to me that these precepts also hark back to those seven maxims which He put at the head of this sermon when He spoke the Beatitudes, and to those seven operations of the Holy Spirit of which the Prophet Isaias makes mention.

As we read on through the treatise we find that all the seven (following Augustine's counting of them) Beatitudes are quoted once more, in their regular order, and at certain intervals as he concludes his discussion of certain sections of the *maiora praecepta*. The following table lists the passages from the Sermon discussed, the space given to them in the treatise, and the paragraph in which each Beatitude is cited:

1) Matt. 5. 21-24 = S. M. 1. 9. 22—10. 28: Blessed are the poor in spirit, 28 fin.
2) Matt. 5. 25 f. = S. M. 1. 11. 29-32: Blessed are the meek, 32 fin.
3) Matt. 5. 27 f. = S. M. 1. 12. 33-36: Blessed are the mourners, 36 fin.
4) Matt. 5. 29-37 = S. M. 1. 13. 1—18. 55: Blessed who hunger and thirst, 54 fin.
5) Matt. 5. 38-48 = S. M. 1. 19. 56—23. 80: Blessed are the merciful, 80 fin.
6) Matt. 6. 1-7. 12 = S. M. 2. 1. 1—22. 76: Blessed are the clean of heart, 76 fin.
7) Matt. 7. 13-23 = S. M. 2. 23. 77—25. 86: Blessed are the peacemakers, 86 fin.

The Beatitudes as cited suit the immediate context. One feels that the author strained somewhat to accommodate them in their order to the text, and that the placing of them results in a rather artificial division of the subject matter of the *maiora praecepta*. A modern commentator would scarcely be inclined to follow it. Augustine seems to sense this himself, writing as he does in the last sentence of this work: 'But whether the order here given should be observed or some other, we must do what we have heard from the Lord if we wish to build on a rock.'

[57a] John 5. 22.

[58] Matt. 4. 11.

[59] Ibid. 8. 12.

[60] Ibid. 25. 23.

[61] *Usque ad faecem.* The phrases *ad faecem, de faece, faece tenus* were often used proverbially in the classical period of Latin (cf. Lucretius 5. 1141; Cicero, *Brut.* 244; Horace, *Carm.* 3. 15. 16); though here *faex* invariably gives expression to something extremely low or despicable (in the same sense, therefore, that we also use the word 'dregs'), rather than the ultimate extent or degree of anything. Cf. A. Otto, *Die Sprichwörter und sprichwörtlichen Redensarten der Römer* (Leipzig 1890) 130 f.

[62] Gen. 3. 19.

[63] Ps. 109. 1.

[64] 1 Cor. 15. 25.

[65] So also Findlay, for *concors—consentiens.* Devoille renders: 'bienveillant'—'d'accord.'

[66] A reference to the *abrenuntiatio Satanae,* the renunciation of Satan, in baptism.

[67] Cf. 2 Cor. 5. 10; Rom. 14. 10.

[68] Cf. Luke 15. 7; also Ps. 50. 19.

[69] James 4. 6.

[70] Eccli. 10. 15.

[71] Ibid. 10. 14.

[72] Rom. 5. 10.

[73] John 5. 22.

[74] Ps. 138. 8-10. The Vulgate has *diluculo,* 'early in the morning' for *in directum,* 'in a straight course.' The latter wording (cf. also Augustine, *Enarr. in Ps.* 138. 12) stems especially from African versions: cf. P. Capelle, *Le texte du Psautier latin en Afrique* (Collect. bibl. lat. 4, Rome 1913) 214.

[75] *Titillari.* Cf. also *Enarr. in Ps.* 143. 6, where Augustine speaks of *delectationis titillatio.*

[76] Gen. 3. From the illustration following, ascribing carnal appetite and pleasure to Eve and reason and consent to Adam, it might be deduced that this contains an intimation of at least a difference of rational endowment in the two sexes and that the stronger endow-

ment is with man. On this matter Augustine states in the *Confessions* (13. 32. 47): ' Just as in his (man's) soul there is one element which rules by deliberation and another which serves obedience, so, too, there was made for man woman in the body, who in her mind indeed possessed an endowment of rational understanding equal to his (*quae haberet quidem in mente rationabilis intelligentiae parem naturam*), but who yet in the sex of her body was subjected to the sex of the man in a way that is like to that by which the impulse to action is in a position of subjection, receiving as it does its capacity to act aright from the reasoning faculty.' Cf. also *De Gen. c. Manich.* 2. 11. 15.

[77] *Ante consuetudinem*, as all manuscripts read except one which has *ante consensionem*.

[78] Cf. 1 Cor. 11. 3 and Eph. 5. 23. For the conclusion of this paragraph, see *Enarr. in Ps.* 143. 6, the comparison of the struggle between the flesh and the spirit, with the life of husband and wife: if the man cedes his rights to his wife and she rules their domestic life, the result is *pax perversa*; but if the wife is subject to her husband and he is in authority, this constitutes *pax recta*.

[79] Mark 5. 41. Here Jesus had ' entered in where the damsel was lying.'

[80] Luke 7. 14. Here the widow's son ' was carried out.'

[81] John 11. 33, 38, 43. Here Lazarus ' had been four days already in the grave '; and Martha said: ' by this time he stinketh.'

[82] Cf. especially Ezech. 16. 20 f.

[83] Col. 3. 5; Eph. 5. 5.

[84] Rom. 7. 24 f.

[85] Augustine has *eat*, ' go,' for the Vulgate *mittatur*, ' be cast.'

[86] Cf. Plautus, *Mil. glor.* 984: *quae te tanquam oculos amat*; Catullus 3. 5: *Quem plus illa oculis suis amabat*; and numerous other examples noted by Otto, *op. cit.*, 249. There also comes to mind the use of the diminutive *ocellus*, e. g., by Catullus, 31. 1 f., addressing Sirmio as *paene insularum insularumque ocelle*. The Bible, too, is not without this comparison; cf. Deut. 32. 10: Invenit eum in terra deserta . . . et custodivit *quasi pupillam oculi sui*; also Ps. 16. 8; Zach. 2. 8; etc.

[87] Deut. 24. 1.

[88] Moses—cf. Deut. 24. 1.

[89] Matt. 19. 8.

[90] Cf. Rom. 7. 2 f. As will be seen in the following, at this time St. Augustine was uncertain concerning the grounds on which the parties

to a marriage could effect a separation. But for him separation never effected a dissolution of marriage. Except for the intervention of death, no remarriage was possible. Cf. especially his *De coniugiis adulterinis* (written in 419). Cf. also below, nn. 119 and 124. For Augustine's teaching on marriage, see J. Peters, *Die Ehe nach der Lehre des hl. Augustinus* (Görres Gesellschaft zur Pflege der Wissenschaft im katholischen Deutschland, Sekt. f. Rechts- u. Sozialwiss. 32, Paderborn 1918); also: B. A. Pereira, *La doctrine du mariage selon saint Augustin* (Etudes de théol. hist., 2nd ed., Paris 1930); A. Reuter, *Sancti Aurelii Augustini doctrina de bonis matrimonii* (Analecta Greg. 27, Rome 1942).

[91] 1 Cor. 7. 10 f.

[92] *Ibid.* 7. 29. Regarding Augustine's views on so-called 'virginal marriage' as also the marriage of Mary and Joseph, cf. Peters, *op. cit.* 4-8.

[93] That is, *parvulorum in Christo*, as the Apostle calls the Corinthians (1 Cor. 3. 1)—'little ones in Christ.'

[94] Luke 14. 26.

[95] Matt. 11. 12.

[96] *Ibid.* 12. 49: 'and stretching forth His hand towards His disciples, He said: Behold my mother and my brethren.' Cf. also Mark 3. 34; also Luke 8. 21.

[97] Gal. 3. 28; also Col. 3. 11.

[98] Matt. 20. 30. Augustine has (so also in *C. Adim.* 25) *neque nubent neque uxores ducent* for *neque nubent neque nubentur* of the Vulgate.

[99] 1 Cor. 15. 53.

[100] Cf. Matt. 22. 30.

[101] In *Retract.* 1. 19. 5 Augustine indicates that here he should not have left the impression that such relations of kinship would not have come into being if death had not intervened as a result of original sin. Relationship of consanguinity and affinity, he states, and increase of the human race would have been had even without original sin and death.

[102] Matt. 6. 9.

[103] Cf. Gal. 4. 27.

[104] St. Augustine speaks of course of the nuptials of Christ and the Church. Cf. 2 Cor. 11. 2; Eph. 5. 22 f. We find this mystical concept in almost all ancient Christian authors; and, as has been said, ' with St. Augustine nuptial Christology reaches its zenith ' (cf. C. Chavasse, *The Bride of Christ* [London 1939] 135). A good collec-

tion of patristic passages on this subject is found in S. Tromp,
"Ecclesia Sponsa Virgo Mater," *Gregorianum* 28 (1937) 3-29.

[105] 1 Cor. 7. 6.

[106] *Ibid.* 7. 29.

[107] Luke 14. 26.

[108] Matt. 6. 25.

[109] Cf. John 10. 15.

[110] The matured Augustine wrote in the *Retractationes* (1. 19. 6):
"Regarding the precept that forbids putting away a wife except on
the ground of fornication, I have here discussed this in minutest
detail. But how the Lord wishes fornication to be understood on the
ground of which one may put away his wife—whether that which is
condemned in lewd acts or that of which it is said: 'Thou hast
destroyed everyone that fornicates from Thee' [Ps. 72. 27: *perdidisti
omnem qui fornicatur abs te*], which surely also includes the former,
for one cannot but 'fornicate' from the Lord, if he 'takes the
members of Christ' and 'makes them the members of an harlot'
[1 Cor. 6. 15]—this must be pondered over and studied again and
again. And in a matter of such importance and so difficult to deter-
mine, I do not wish the reader to think that this our discussion of it
should suffice him. But let him also read elsewhere either what we
have written at a later period, or what others have investigated and
dealt with better than we; or, if he is equal to the task, let him
himself put his mind with superior keenness and comprehension to
what can rightly be regarded as problems here. No, not every sin
is fornication—admittedly God does not destroy every sinner, who
daily deigns to hear His saints say: 'Forgive us our debts' [Matt.
6. 12], whereas He destroys everyone who 'fornicates' from Him.
But what is to be understood as fornication and how the term is to
be delimited, whether even because of it one may put away his wife
is a question full of pitfalls. That it is permitted by reason of that
fornication which is committed in lewd actions, there can be no
question. Again, where I said that this was permitted, but not
ordered, I did not note another Scripture saying: 'He that keepeth
an adulteress is foolish and wicked' [Prov. 18. 22]. And of course
I would not say that that woman should have been regarded as an
adulteress even after she heard from the Lord: 'Neither will I. Go,
and now sin no more' [John 8. 11], if on hearing this she obeyed.

[111] 1 Cor. 7. 10 f.

[112] *Ibid.* 7. 11.

[113] John 8. 11: *Vade, et vide deinceps ne pecces;* the Vulgate reads: *Vade, et iam amplius noli peccare.*

[114] 1 Cor. 7. 4.

[115] *Ibid.* 7. 12.

[116] *Ibid.*

[117] *Ibid.* 7. 13.

[118] *Ibid.* 7. 25 f.

[119] *Ibid.* 7. 6. St. Augustine in this section permits a separation in any case, not requiring the conditions set for the granting of the so-called Pauline Privilege today: namely, that the non-Christian party refuses to convert and to cohabit peacefully with the converted party. But to all appearances Augustine's more liberal attitude provides for only a *dimissio,* separation, in such cases and not the permission to remarry; whereas in the eyes of the Church the application of the Privilege nullifies the marriage and remarriage is permissible. For the pertinent passages in Augustine, cf. Peters, *op. cit.* 68-71; Pereira, *op. cit.* 141-48.

[120] 1 Cor. 7. 14. Augustine reads *in uxore—in fratre;* the Vulgate, *per mulierem fidelem—per virum fidelem.*

[121] *Ibid.*

[122] *Sanctificati erant,* that is, 'had been made Christians' through the conferring of baptism and the reception of the Gifts of the Holy Ghost. For the meaning of *sanctificatus* = 'Christian,' 'believer,' and *sanctitas* = 'being a Christian,' 'Christianity,' cf. S. W. J. Teeuwen, *Sprachlicher Bedeutungswandel bei Tertullian* (Stud. z. Gesch. u. Kultur d. Altert. 14. 1, Paderborn 1926) 98 f.

[123] Luke 10. 35.

[124] Cf. above, n. 110, Augustine's admission that he later doubted seriously the validity of these conclusions. Cf. Peters, *op. cit.* 48 f. The author points out that even in the *Retractationes* Augustine's restriction of the term 'fornication' as a ground for separation to its normal scope of application is insufficient. He is probably right in stating that apparently even the great bishop of Hippo was to some extent influenced by his surroundings and times—the Roman world in which no bond was more readily unbound than the marriage bond. But for Augustine there was only separation—no divorce or remarriage as long as both parties were alive!

[125] Rom. 2. 1.

[125a] Only death can break their marriage bond, as Augustine states later—*De bono coni.* 34. 32: *nec solvitur vinculum nuptiale nisi coniugis morte.*

[126] Cf. Gen. 16. 1 ff., the case of Abraham taking Agar at the suggestion of his barren wife Sara.

[127] Here St. Augustine refers briefly to his doctrine of certain stages or epochs—*aetates*—through which man has passed since the Creation. Sometimes these *aetates* number four, sometimes six. Cf., for example, *Enchir.* 31. 118 f. (see L. A. Arand, ACW 3 [1947] 109 f. and 146 n. 384); *De Cat. rud.* 22. 39 (see J. P. Christopher, ACW 2 [1946] 70 f. and 136 nn. 249 and 250); *De Trin.* 4. 4. 7; *De civ. Dei* 22. 30.

[128] 1 Cor. 7. 4.

[129] Septimius Acindynus (= ἀκίνδυνος)—not 'Acyndinus,' as the manuscripts read in the present passage—was a Roman governor of the Orient (*praefectus praetoris Orientis*) from 338 to 340 and consul in 340. Cf. W. Liebenam, *Fasti consulares Imperii Romani von 30 v. Chr. bis 565 n. Chr.* (Bonn 1910) 36; also O. Seeck, Pauly-Wissowa, RE 1 (1893) s. v. "Akindynos 3." Considering that St. Augustine wrote the present treatise probably in the year 394 and that Acindynus was governor from 338 to 340, the author's statement that the incident with its Solomonic climax took place *ante quinquaginta ferme annos* is quite correct.

Concerning Augustine's uncertain attitude in respect to the moral issues involved in this narrative (cf. also below: 'Out of this story I make no argument of any sort. Let each one pass judgment as he wishes'), cf. Peters, *op. cit.* 26. Peters makes the point that at this time Augustine obviously was not clear on the contractual nature of marriage; that in the marriage contract the parties are not free to give up or transfer their rights, because these rights have been fixed by God *ab initio*.

[130] Cf. Lev. 19. 12; also Exod. 20, Num. 30. 3, Deut. 5. 11.

[131] Gal. 1. 20.

[132] 2 Cor. 11. 31.

[133] Rom. 1. 9 f.

[134] 1 Cor. 15. 31.

[135] Νὴ τὴν καύχησιν ὑμετέραν. When Joseph was interrogating his brothers who had come to Egypt to purchase food he commanded that their youngest brother Benjamin be brought, twice using the oath νὴ τὴν ὑγίειαν Φαραώ, 'by the health of Pharao.' For an appreciation of St. Augustine's assiduous attention to the Greek text of the Bible, see D. De Bruyne, "Saint Augustin reviseur de la Bible," *Miscellanea Agostiniana* 2 (Rome 1931) 521-606.

[136] Matt. 6. 13.

[137] St. Augustine often discusses the habit of swearing: *C. Fortun. Man.* 2. 22; *De mend.* 28; *Serm.* 308. 3. 2: 'Prius ergo laborare debetis, et confligere adversus consuetudinem vestram malam, malam, malam, et valde malam.' Augustine states that before his conversion he himself was given to the habit (*Serm.* 180. 9. 10): 'Iuravimus et nos passim, habuimus istam teterrimam consuetudinem et mortiferam. Dico caritati vestrae: ex quo Deo servire coepimus, timuimus vehementer et veternosissimam consuetudinem timore frenavimus.'

[138] 1 Cor. 2. 15.

[139] Gen. 3. 19.

[140] Confugiens ad arcem *Christianae militiae.* Already Job had said (7. 1): *Militia est vita hominis super terram,* 'The life of man upon earth is a warfare.' The ancient Christian writers, in many instances living in times of persecutions, and witnesses, or themselves sufferers of martyrdom, were fond of speaking of the Christian's spiritual struggles in terms of the military profession. Cf. the celebrated study by A. Harnack, *Militia Christi: die christliche Religion und der Soldatenstand in den ersten drei Jahrhunderten* (Leipzig 1905); also the literature listed by J. P. Christopher in his translation of St. Augustine's *De catechizandis rudibus,* ACW 2 (1946) 148 f.

[141] *Vestimentum* for *pallium* in the Vulgate; cf. below, n. 155.

[142] St. Augustine's interpretation is quite identical in sense with the words of modern commentators; cf., for example, A. H. M'Neile, *The Gospel According to St. Matthew* (London 1915): 'The law of the *ius talionis,* like that of divorce (see *v.* 31), was restrictive rather than permissive; it limited revenge by fixing an exact compensation for an injury.'

[143] *Pro temporum distributione*—evidently another reference to Augustine's theory of the divinely planned periodicity of man's history: cf. above, n. 127.

[144] Christ as our physician—always a popular concept with the Fathers—was so referred to already by Ignatius of Antioch: *Ephes.* 7. 2. Especially in his sermons St. Augustine often speaks of Christ as *medicus animarum* and of His healing activity in our souls as *sanatio, curatio.* Christ's purpose in coming to earth, he states (*Enarr. in Ps.* 35. 17), was 'to heal man's wounds of pride.' That man might not recoil from tribulations the patient suffering of which is a condition for the curing of all the ailments of his sins, 'He, the Physician, drank the bitter medicine first' (*ibid.* 98. 3). Moreover, this physician is omnipotent—*omnipotens medicus.* In His practice there are no incurable diseases; and He charges no fee (*ibid.* 102. 5 f.) Cf.

ibid. 94. 7; *Serm.* 87. 10. 13 ff.; 88. 1. 1 ff.; 3. 7 Frang. (206 Morin); etc. For the priest regarded as a physician of souls, see especially Gregory of Nazianzus, *Or.* 2. 16-34; cf. M. J. Suelzer's observations, ACW 4 (1947) 183.

[145] 2 Cor. 11. 20 f.

[146] Cf. *ibid.* 12. 15.

[147] Cf. Acts 22. 25. Paul of Tarsus was born a Roman citizen (cf. Acts 22. 28). Readers of the Acts will compare St. Paul's celebrated appeal, CIVIS SUM ROMANUS, with its classical counterpart in their college Latin reading: Cicero, *The Verrine Orations* 5. 147, 158 ff. Here, to quote Cicero (162): 'caedebatur virgis in medio foro Messanae civis Romanus, iudices, cum interea nullus gemitus, nulla vox alia illius miseri inter dolorem crepitumque plagarum audiebatur, nisi haec: CIVIS SUM ROMANUS.' Why, when Paul and Silas—both Roman citizens—were being scourged (Acts 16. 22), they did not utter this cry, has never been satisfactorily explained. Cf. A. Steinmann, *Die Apostelgeschichte* (Die hl. Schrift 4, 4th ed., Bonn 1934) 193. Later, in the times of persecution, this cry of appeal to Roman citizenship was to yield its lustre to the proud cry of admission of Christian citizenship and suzerainty—CHRISTIANUS SUM. Cf. especially Tertullian, *Apol.* 2.

[148] For another instance of a detailed exposition of the right and left as symbolical of eternal and temporal values, read *Enarr. in Ps.* 136. 15 f.—a discussion of Ps. 136. 5: 'If I forget thee, O Jerusalem, let my right hand be forgotten.'

[149] Acts 23. 3.

[150] *Ibid.* 23. 5.

[151] Ps. 56. 8.

[152] John 18. 23.

[153] According to St. Augustine, slavery is not a natural state but one that rose as a punishment for sin. In this sense it was ordained by the same law that commands the preservation of the natural order and prohibits interference with it; cf. *De civ. Dei* 19. 15. For this latter passage, see J. Mausbach, *Die Ethik des heiligen Augustinus* (2nd ed., Freiburg i. Br. 1929) 1. 327 f.

[154] In *De civ. Dei* 19. 16 Augustine emphasizes that it is the master's duty to lead his slaves with the same affection—*pari dilectione*—that he bestows upon his sons and daughters, to the worship of God, *ad Deum colendum.*

[155] Throughout this section Augustine has rendered the word

ἱμάτιον in Matt. 5. 40 with *vestimentum* ('let go thy *garment* also'), whereas the Vulgate reads *pallium* ('let go thy cloak also'). The two articles of clothing mentioned in the Gospel—the coat (χιτών *tunica*) and the cloak (ἱμάτιον, *pallium*)—were essential pieces in the Orient. According to St. Matthew, Our Lord states that if we are sued for the former, we are also to surrender the more valuable piece, the cloak. Cf. M'Neile, *op. cit.* 70; also A. Durand, *Evangile selon Saint Matthieu* (Verbum Salutis 1, 3rd ed., Paris 1929) 93. Augustine, however, appears to have understood ἱμάτιον as used in the sense of *vestimentum*—any other piece of clothing or a garment. Some, he adds at the end, gave this a specific interpretation, thinking of a cloak—*pallium*—as the most likely other *vestimentum* owned by the accused. Among the *nonnulli* referred to by Augustine there was of course St. Jerome who had revised the Gospels a decade before (383). Incidentally, at about the same time that the *De sermone Domini in Monte* was written, in 394, Augustine himself also wrote *pallium* in quoting Matt. 5. 40: cf. *C. Adim.* 8.

[155a] For Augustine the number "3" (*ternarius numerus*) was also particularly significant as it designated the Trinity: cf. *Serm.* 252. 10: *Ternarius vero numerus conditorem Patrem et Filium et Spiritum Sanctum insinuat; Ep.* 55. 11. 20, 31. Regarding Augustine's love for numbers, cf. M. C. D'Arcy, "The Philosophy of St. Augustine," *A Monument to St. Augustine* (London 1930) 169-71; 192 f. See below, 203 n. 92.

[156] Prov. 3. 12, according to the Septuagint; cf. also Heb. 12. 6.

[157] Luke 12. 47 f. Augustine reverses the order of the verses, as he does again in *Serm.* 1. 133. 11 Bibl. Casin. (408 Morin).

[158] Cf. 3 Kings 18. 40 and 4 Kings 1. 10.

[159] Cf. Luke 9. 51-56. .

[160] Cf. John 15. 26 and Acts 2. 1-4.

[161] Cf. Acts 5. 1-10.

[162] The heretics referred to are evidently the Manichaeans. Their rejection of the Old Testament was notorious. For their opposition to the Acts of the Apostles, cf. Augustine, *C. epist. Manich.* 10. 11; *C. Faust. Manich.* 32. 15 f. Augustine was at this time writing his anti-Manichaean treatises.

[163] 1 Cor. 5. 5—the case of a man who had married his stepmother or was keeping her as his mistress.

[164] Cf. the apocryphal *Acts of Thomas* 6-9, in the translation by M. R. James, *The Apocryphal New Testament* (Oxford 1924) 367 f. For the esteem in which these Acts were held by the Manichaeans,

see again Augustine, C. *Faust. Manich.* 22. 79; *C. Adimant. Manich.*
17. 2 (here the incident related above is given in greater detail).

[165] Cf. above, nn. 127 and 143.

[166] 2 Cor. 9. 7.

[167] Augustine here follows the Greek tradition which does not
have 'and calumniate' after 'that persecute,' as does the Vulgate.
In the following he reads 'who commandeth (*iubet*) His sun,' but
further down, 23. 79., he has 'who maketh (*facit*) His sun,' which
is also the reading of the Vulgate.

[168] Cf. Matt. 5. 17.

[169] Here the author commits an inaccuracy. The first part of the
Lord's citation in Matt. 5. 43—*Thou shalt love thy neighbor*—is found
in Lev. 19. 18. The second part, however— *and hate thy enemy*—is
found nowhere in the Mosaic Law. It is rather an inference that
could be made from the fact that the Old Testament law distinguished
between conduct toward a fellow Israelite and toward a non-Israelite
or Gentile. In Leviticus the Jew had been commanded to love his
own people; but as to his non-Jewish neighbors, the pagans—
Moabites, for example, and Ammonites—he was told (Deut. 23. 6):
'Thou shalt not make peace with them, neither shalt thou seek their
prosperity all the days of thy life forever.' Some peoples he had
even been commanded to destroy entirely (Exod. 17. 14-16; Deut.
7. 1 ff., etc.). It is quite probable that some Jewish teachers, drawing
their own conclusions from these divine ordinances, had actually
'supplemented' the command, *Thou shalt love thy neighbor*, with
the very words, *and hate thy enemy*. And this may have led to an
attempted justification of even personal enmities. At any rate, the
oft-quoted sentence by the Roman historian Tacitus (*Hist.* 5. 5) may
be quoted again as characterizing the Jewish hatred of national
enemies even so late as the second century A. D.: 'They are fanati-
cally loyal among themselves and always ready to compassionate
their own, but all other peoples they hate as enemies.' St. Paul, too,
calls them *adversaries of all men* (1 Thess. 2. 15). For further discussion of Matt. 5. 43, cf. M'Neile, *op. cit.* 71; Durand, *op. cit.* 94-
96; W. C. Allen, *A Critical and Exegetical Commentary of the
Gospel according to St. Matthew* (Int. Crit. Comm., New York
1907) 55; A. Fernandez, "Diligite inimicos vestros," *Verbum Domini*
1 (1921) 39-42; L. F. Miller, *The Gospel According to Saint
Matthew* (New York 1937) 110 f.; etc.

[170] Ps. 68. 23.

[171] *Ibid.* 108. 9.

[172] Rom. 12. 14.

[173] Matt. 11. 20-24; Luke 10. 13-15.

[174] 2 Tim. 4. 14, concerning Alexander the coppersmith.

[175] Actually the Gospels read (Matt. 11. 21 and Luke 10. 13):
'Woe to thee, *Corozain!* Woe to thee, Bethsaida!' Capharnaum is
mentioned later (Matt. 11. 23): 'And thou, Capharnaum, shalt
thou be exalted up to heaven? Thou shalt go down even unto hell.'

[176] *Merito infidelitatis = propter infidelitatem.*

[177] Acts 23. 3; cf. above, 19. 58. Augustine seems to imply that
Paul foresaw the destruction of Jerusalem in the year 70. The incident referred to took place before the Sanhedrin in the year 58; St.
Paul's words were directed to the high priest Ananias who had
given orders to strike him in the face.

[178] Ps. 2. 1.

[179] St. Augustine's use of the preterite tense—'have raged' (*fre-
muerunt*) and 'have devised' (*meditati sunt*)—corresponds to the
same usage in the Septuagint and the Vulgate, which for the Psalms
is a mere translation of the Septuagint. However, in the Septuagint
the utter inadequacy of the tenses as mechanically rendered from the
original Hebrew is notorious; and Augustine's argument from prophe-
cies made in terms of the past rests on a correspondingly weak
basis. In the present passage the new translation of the Psalter issued
by the Pontifical Biblical Institute in 1945 uses the present tense for
the perfect: 'Why are the Gentiles in uproar (*tumultuantur*) and
why do the people devise (*meditantur*) vain things?' Regarding the
problem of tenses in the Psalms, cf. A. Bea, "The New Psalter: Its
Origin and Spirit," *Cath. Bibl. Quarterly* 8 (1946) 17 f.

[180] Ps. 21. 19. Here again the new version uses the present tense:
'they part' (*dividunt*), 'they cast lots' (*mittunt sortem*).

[181] 1 John 5. 16. The Vulgate has 'life shall be given to him'
for 'the Lord shall give life to him.'

[182] 1 Cor. 7. 14.

[183] *Ibid.* 7. 15.

[184] In the *Retractationes* 1. 19. 7, Augustine states that he should
have added: '—if he ends this life in such heinous perversity of
mind.' He remarks further that, no matter how wicked any man is
in his lifetime, we certainly must not despair of him; and we do well
to pray for one whom we do not abandon to despair.

[185] Luke 23. 34.

[186] Acts 7. 59.

[187] 2 Tim. 4. 14-16.

[188] Cf. Matt. 18. 21 f. and Luke 17. 3 f.

[189] Matt. 27. 4.

[190] Cf. Matt. 12. 32.

[191] Cf. *ibid.* 12. 24; Mark 3. 22.

[192] Matt. 10. 25.

[193] *Ibid.* 12. 32.

[194] *Ibid.* 12. 33. Regarding the sin against the Holy Spirit, St. Augustine states in a sermon (*Serm.* 71. 5. 8) delivered probably in the year 417 that 'in all Sacred Scripture perhaps no greater, no more difficult question can be found.' Cf. also *Ep.* 185.

[195] Rom. 12. 14, 17.

[196] Cf. Apoc. 6. 10.

[197] In *Enarr. in Ps.* 30, *serm.* 3. 2, St. Augustine states that 'the enemies against whom we are to pray are the devil and his angels.'

[198] Rom. 6. 12.

[199] 1 Cor. 9. 26 f.

[200] John 1. 12.

[201] Cf. Rom. 8. 16 f.; Gal. 4. 5-7.

[202] Wisd. 7. 26.

[203] Mal. 4. 2. There is a strange duplication here: 'the sun of justice is risen (*ortus est*) unto me,' 'the sun of justice shall arise' (*orietur*). The first quotation does not occur anywhere in the Bible. Perhaps there is a reminiscence of Ps. 71. 7: 'In his days shall justice spring up' (*orietur*). Regarding Christ as the *sol iustitiae*, see F. J. Dölger, *Die Sonne der Gerechtigkeit und der Schwarze* (Liturgiegesch. Forsch. 2, Münster i. W. 1918) 100-110.

[204] Wisd. 5. 6.

[205] Isa. 5. 6.

[206] Gen. 1. 2, 16.

[207] Osee 6. 6. The Vulgate: 'I desired mercy, and not sacrifice.'

[208] Here it is quite impossible effectively to imitate the play of words: *misericors* (merciful)—*miseria* (misery), followed by the words within the Scripture citations: *misericordiam, misericordes, miserebitur.*

BOOK TWO

[1] Here and in the following the phrases *simplex oculus* ('single eye') and *simplex cor* ('single heart') are Scriptural; for the former, cf. Matt. 6. 22; Luke 11. 34; for the latter, Gen. 20. 6; 2 Kings 15. 11; Job 33. 3; 1 Peter 1. 22. Cf. C. Spicq, "La vertu du simplicité dans l'Ancien et le Nouveau Testament," *Rev. de théol. et de phil.* 22 (1930) 1-26.

[2] Ps. 33. 3.

[3] Gal. 1. 10.

[4] 1Cor. 10. 32 f. In the original text the first part of this quotation reads very different: 'Be without offense.' Elsewhere, for example, in his *De op. monach.* 13. 14, Augustine gives the original wording.

[5] Phil. 4. 17.

[6] Augustine here adverts to the original meaning of *hypocrita*, ὑποκριτής: an impersonator on the stage, player, actor. The word appears to have been first used by the writer of comedies, Aristophanes (cf. *Vesp.* 1279). The derived meaning, one who feigns virtue or piety in order to obtain the approbation of others, apparently occurs first in the Gospels. The word is found in the Septuagint (Job 34. 30; 36. 13), but here it is used for a wicked, impious person. Cf. T. Ortolan, "Hypocrisie," *Dict. de théol. cath.* 7. 1 (1930) 365-69; P. Joüon, "Ὑποκριτής dans l'Evangile," *Rech. de science rel.* 20 (1930) 312-17.

[7] *Suspector cordis*: cf. Prov. 24. 12. In Wisd. 1. 6 God is called *scrutator cordis*.

[8] Luke 13. 27. (Augustine has *operarii dolosi* for *operarii iniquitatis*); cf. also Ps. 6. 9 and Matt. 7. 23.

[9] Cf. Acts 3 and 4.

[10] Prov. 25. 21, but cited from the quotation in Rom. 12. 20.

[11] Cf. 1 Cor. 7. 13-17.

[12] Our modern critical editions of the New Testament produce evidence that some of the Greek codices, for example, two preserved at Paris, do have 'openly'—ἐν τῷ φανερῷ; and certain manuscripts of the so-called *Vetus Latina* have the corresponding word *palam*. Regarding this passage and others to follow below (9. 30; 22. 74), D. De Bruyne points out that they indicate that Augustine in many instances corrected the pre-Vulgate text of the Gospels on the basis

of the Greek original; cf. De Bruyne, "Saint Augustin reviseur de la Bible," *Miscellanea Agostiniana* 2 (Rome 1931) 594-602.

[13] Ps. 4. 5.

[14] The picture represents the invading of one's private quarters. *Cubiculum* in Matt. 6. 6 (Isa. 26. 20) is a bedroom; in the Greek text ταμεῖον = an inner room, a sanctum.

[15] *Ita ethnicorum, id est, gentilium.* There are other passages in which Augustine explains the term *ethnicus* (ἐθνικός), for example *Serm.* 17. 66; *Ethnicus gentilis est;* 82. 4. 7: Nam et ipsos *ethnicos, id est, gentiles et paganos.* From this C. Mohrmann, *Die altchristliche Sondersprache in den Sermones des hl. Augustinus* (Lat. Christ. prim. 3, Nijmegen 1932) 110, rightly deduces that the term was uncommon in Augustine's time. Moreover, it occurs rather seldom in his works, whereas *gentilis* and *paganus* occur constantly. On the other hand, Tertullian, to whom the Latin of early Christianity owed so much, had used the word *ethnicus* very often.

[16] *Multiloquium,* the word used in the verse just quoted from St. Matthew: 'much speaking.' Augustine here evidently has in mind the cultivation of rhetoric and eloquence among the Greeks and Romans. 'Eloquence,' by the way, is the rendering given by R. A. Knox for the word *multiloquium* in Matthew.

[17] Cf. Matt. 23. 10.

[18] This version of the Lord's Prayer contains two striking divergences from its form in the Vulgate: 'Give us this day our *daily* bread' and '*bring* us not into temptation.' Concerning these— also to be referred to again below (nn. 49 and 68)—cf. the very informative remarks by L. A. Arand in his translation of Saint Augustine's *Faith, Hope, and Charity*: ACW 3 (1947) 145 n. 377. Regarding Augustine's various discussions of the Lord's Prayer, cf. J. Moffatt, "Augustine on the Lord's Prayer," *Expositor* 18 (1919) 259-72. One of the finest modern treatments of the *Oratio Dominica* is by R. Guardini, *Das Gebet des Herrn* (2nd ed., Tübingen 1934). For a list of the principal patristic discussions of this prayer and for recent literature, cf. M. Viller-K. Rahner, *Aszese und Mystik in der Väterzeit* (Freiburg i. Br. 1938) 292-95; also E. Vykoukal, "Vater Unser," *Lex. f. Theol. u. Kirche* 10 (1938) 501.

[19] Isa. 1. 2.

[20] Ps. 81. 6.

[21] Mal. 1. 6. The order of the questions is inverted.

[22] John 1. 12.

[23] Gal. 4. 1.

[24] Rom. 8. 15.

[25] Cf. *ibid.* 8. 17 and 23.

[26] Ps. 33. 19.

[27] Gen. 3. 19.

[28] 1 Cor. 3. 17; cf. also *ibid.* 6. 19 and 2 Cor. 6. 16.

[29] Here Saint Augustine mentions two very interesting and significant liturgical practices connected with prayer in ancient Christianity:
it was said standing and facing the east. For the former, the standing
position, see, for example, *Apost. Const.* 2. 57. 14; Gregory of Nazianzus, *Ep.* 34; Cyprian, *De dom. orat.* 31 (Quando autem stamus ad
orationem . . .). Cf. F. J. Dölger, *Sol Salutis: Gebet und Gesang im
christlichen Altertum, mit besonderer Rücksicht auf die Ostung in
Gebet und Liturgie* (Liturgiegesch. Forsch. 4. 5, 2nd ed., Münster
i. W. 1925) 325 f.; also *ibid.*, the entries in the index under 'Stehen
beim Gebet.' Orientation, the practice of facing the east during
prayer and worship, was common among the ancients: e. g. the
Egyptians, Thracians, Persians (cf. Tertullian, *Apol.* 16. 11), etc.
From primitive times the rising of the sun in the east and its setting
in the west was associated with good and evil, life and death, joy and
sorrow. We need but recall the prevalence of sun worship in the
history of mankind to understand the significance attached to speaking prayer in the direction of the sun's daily reappearance. Ancient
Christianity retained the custom of facing the east during prayer but
gave a new, Christian significance to the practice. The terrestrial
Paradise lay to the east (Gen. 2. 8: κατὰ ἀνατολάς) and the celestial
Paradise of the blessed was believed to be in the east since Christ's
ascension had taken place 'to the east' (Ps. 67. 34); so, too, the final
'coming of the Son of man' was placed in the east (cf. Matt. 24. 27).
The patristic texts for this orientation in prayer are very numerous:
cf. Tertullian, *Ad nat.* 1. 13; *Apol.* 16. 9-11; Clement of Alexandria,
Strom. 7. 7. 43-6; Origen, *In Num. hom.* 5. 1; Basil, *De Spir. Sanc.*
27. 66; etc. On the subject, see Dölger, *op. cit.*, passim; H. Leclercq,
"Orientation," *Dict. d'archéol. chrét. et de liturgie* 12. 2 (1936)
2665-69; J. Sauer, "Ostung," *Lex. f. Theol. u. Kirche* 7 (1935) 826-
28; A. C. Rush, *Death and Burial in Christian Antiquity* (Stud. in
Christ. Ant. 1, Washington 1941) 36 f., 60 f., 66. f.

[30] The sun; cf. the preceding note.

[31] Ps. 75. 1.

[31a] Here there is an echo of the triumphant march of Christianity
since the proclamation of the Edict of Milan by Constantine the
Great in the year 313. In Augustine's own time the measures of the
emperors Gratian (375-83) and Theodosius the Great (379-95)

made this triumph complete. Paganism was doomed everywhere—it was Christianity's classical period of mass conversions.

[32] Matt. 24. 14.

[33] *Homo Dominicus*: the adjective has the force of a genitive, ' of the Lord '; cf. J. Schrijnen-C. Mohrmann, *Studien zur Syntax der Briefe des hl. Cyprian* 1 (Lat. Christ. prim. 5, Nijmegen 1936) 91-93, 96-99. Later, in the *Retractationes* 1. 19. 8, Augustine expresses his displeasure with having used this term—*homo dominicus*: " I fail to see that it is correct to call Him ' man of the Lord ' who is the Mediator between God and man, the man Christ Jesus, when certainly He is the Lord. And as to ' man of the Lord '—who is there in His sacred household who cannot be called such? And as for my using this expression, I found it in my reading of some of the commentaries of the Sacred Scriptures. At any rate, wherever I may have used the term, I wish I had not used it. In later years I realized that it should not be used, even though something may be said for it."

[34] John 6. 45; cf. Isa. 54. 13.

[35] Matt. 22. 30.

[36] *In caelestem habitationem atque immutationem . . . assumendi* (cf. 1 Cor. 15. 52).

[37] Luke 2. 14.

[38] John 4. 34.

[39] *Ibid.* 6. 38; cf. *ibid.* 5. 30; Matt. 26. 39; Luke 22. 42.

[40] Matt. 12. 49 f.

[41] Cf. *ibid.* 25. 31-46.

[42] Rom. 7. 25.

[43] 1 Cor. 15. 54, 53.

[44] Cf. *ibid.* 15. 52: '. . . and we shall be changed ' (*immutabimur*).

[45] Rom. 7. 18.

[46] *Ibid.* 7. 22.

[47] Throughout ancient Christianity the Church is personified as a woman, a virgin (*virgo*)—as the bride (*sponsa*) and the wife (*uxor, mulier*) of Christ who begets children (*filios generat*) and thus becomes our mother (*Mater Ecclesia, mater nostra*). For modern studies on this subject, cf. C. Chavasse, *The Bride of Christ: An Enquiry into the Nuptial Element in Early Christianity* (London 1939); S. Tromp, " Ecclesia Sponsa Virgo Mater," *Gregorianum* 28 (1937) 3-29; J. C. Plumpe, *Mater Ecclesia: An Inquiry into the Concept of the Church as Mother in Early Christianity* (Stud. in Christ. Ant. 5, Washington 1943). For Augustine, see also F. Hof-

mann, *Der Kirchenbegriff des hl. Augustinus* (Munich 1933), esp. 263-75. The prototypes for the Church's brideship and motherhood were already present in the Scriptures: see Plumpe, *op. cit.* 1-8.

[48] The conception of the earth as a woman (Augustine here: *quasi femina*) and mother and the divinization of the earth as such— *Terra Mater, Γαῖα Παμμήτειρα*, etc.—belongs to primitive history; cf. esp. A. Dieterich, *Mutter Erde, ein Versuch über Volksreligion* (3rd ed. by E. Fehrle, Leipzig 1925). Such personification is also found in the Old Testament: the Book of Ecclesiasticus (40. 1) speaks of man's burial into the mother of all (*in matrem omnium*).

[49] The Vulgate reads ' our supersubstantial bread' (*panem nostrum supersubstantialem*). This is a change made by St. Jerome from the older Latin version here followed by St. Augustine: 'our daily bread' (*panem nostrum quotidianum*). Jerome retained this latter reading—the one we follow when saying the Our Father—in Luke 11. 3, although in both Matthew and Luke the Greek original uses the same modifier for 'bread,' the much-debated word ἐπιούσιος.

[50] Matt. 6. 34.

[51] Augustine often speaks of daily Holy Communion, especially in his sermons. He states (*In Ioan. Ev. tract.* 26. 15) that in his time Communion was received ' *alicubi quotidie, alicubi certis intervallis dierum* ': ' in some places daily, in other places at certain intervals.' Cf. also *Ep.* 54 (*Ad Ianuarium*) 2: ' *Alii quotidie communicant corpori et sanguini Domini, alii certis diebus accipiunt.*' His own attitude in this matter is reflected in an Easter sermon (*Serm.* 227) in which he admonishes the newly-baptized concerning the reception of the Eucharist: ' You should realize what you have received, what you will receive in the future, what you ought to receive daily.' Convenient access to these and similar passages in Augustine is offered by P. Browe, *De frequenti communione in Ecclesia Occidentali usque ad annum c. 1000 documenta varia* (Text. et doc., ser. theol. 5, Rome 1932) 18-23; however, add to this collection *Serm.* 9. 1 Wilmart (693 Morin). Cf. also below, n. 56.

[52] John 6. 27.

[53] *Ibid.* 6. 41.

[54] Luke 12. 22; cf. also Matt. 6. 31.

[55] Luke 12. 31.

[56] For the East of the third century we have testimony that at least in Egypt Holy Communion was received daily; cf. Clement of Alexandria, *Quis dives salvetur* 23; Origen, *In Gen. hom.* 10. In

the fourth century Basil recommends daily reception, stating that he himself communicates at least four times a week (*Ep.* 93). But after him we find John Chrysostom complaining that at Constantinople many received Communion only once a year: cf. *In Ep. ad Heb. hom.* 17. 4; *In Ep. ad Tim. hom.* 5. 3. According to Cassian (*Collat.* 22. 21), the abbot Theonas stated that in Egypt some monks communicated no oftener than once yearly. This diffidence towards frequent reception arose from an exaggerated respect for the Sacrament, which in turn had been engendered especially by the great stress placed upon the divinity of Christ in combating Arianism. Cf. E. Dublanchy, "Communion fréquente," *Dict. de théol. cath.* 3. 1 (1939) 515-21. In the West, St. Ambrose challenged such diffidence and abstention: 'One who is not worthy to receive daily, is not worthy to receive after a year' (*De sacr.* 5. 4. 25). Cf. J. Quasten, *Monumenta eucharistica et liturgica vetustissima* (Bonn 1935) 169. For the practice of the West during the first millenium of Christianity, cf. the materials gathered by Browe, *op. cit.* Cf. also V. Mariani, *Sulla communione dottrina dei Padri e antica disciplina della Chiesa* (Chiavari 1905).

[57] Heb. 3. 13: *quandiu dicitur*; Vulgate = *donec hodie cognominatur.*

[58] Ps. 94. 8.

[59] Heb. 3. 13; cf. above, n. 57.

[60] Matt. 5. 26.

[61] Cf. Luke 13. 1-4. Regarding the second example, which is the first in Luke's report, Augustine is inaccurate on two points: he confuses Pilate with Herod, and those slain are not called 'debtors' (*debitores*) but 'sinners' (*peccatores*).

[62] *Ibid.* 13. 5.

[63] Matt. 5. 40; cf. above, 1. 19. 59 f.

[64] 2 Tim. 2. 24.

[65] The word *corrigere* is used. The obligation of striving to bring an erring fellow Christian round to doing what is right—fraternal correction, *correctio* (*correptio*) *fraterna*—is inculcated by St. Augustine everywhere in his writings. He stated earlier in the present treatise (1. 20. 66) that correction must not be shunned, that in bringing it to bear we are to use progressively advice (*consilium*), authority (*auctoritas*), and force (*potestas*). Of course, this correction is a duty implied in the command to love our neighbor as ourself (cf. above, 20. 64). In exercising this obligation we must ever be careful not to substitute a penchant for vituperation and

condemnation of others for virtuous, unselfish efforts to bring the other person to better ways (cf. below, 2. 19. 63). St. Augustine, moreover, wrote a work, *De correptione et gratia*, in which he shows that correction must be made in numerous situations, even though in every instance a man's betterment is dependent upon divine grace. As he himself states (*Retract.* 2. 67), he wrote this book to refute the contention that correction is not necessary and that the only thing we can do for another when he transgresses God's commands, is to pray for him.

The duty of fraternal correction is stressed already in the *Didache* 15. 3: 'Correct one another, not in anger, but in composure, as you have it in the Gospel.' The reference is to Matt. 18. 15-18; the translation is by J. A. Kleist, Ms. of ACW 6.

⁶⁶ Matt. 5. 44; cf. above, chapters 21 and 22 of the first book.

⁶⁷ Book 1, chapters 19 and 20.

⁶⁸ St. Augustine consistently used *inferas* ('bring into') for *inducas* ('lead into'), St. Jerome's version in the Vulgate of εἰσενέγκῃς. Regarding this and literature on the subject, cf. L. A. Arand, ACW 3 (1947) 145 n. 377.

⁶⁹ St. Cyprian, for example, used this form: *ne patiaris nos induci in tentationem*; cf. *De dom. orat.* 7, 25. Cf. Arand, *loc. cit.*

⁷⁰ Eccli. 34. 11 (cf. also 9). Augustine here uses *tentare, tentatio* throughout. *Tentare* originally means 'to put to trial,' 'try,' 'test.' But already Cicero uses the word in the sense of 'to tempt': cf. *In Verr. act.* 2. 1. 105.

⁷¹ Gal. 4. 13 f.

⁷² Deut. 13. 3; the Vulgate has 'that it may appear' (*ut palam fiat*) for 'that He may know' (*ut sciat*).

⁷³ *Dies laetus,* e. g., Cicero, *De amic.* 3. 12; *In Vatin.* 6; Ovid, *Fast.* 1. 87: 'Salve, *laeta dies!*'

⁷⁴ *Frigus pigrum,* e. g., Tibullus 1. 2. 29. This apparently was used in schools of rhetoric to illustrate the figure of metonymy: cf. *Rhet. ad Her.* 4. 32. 43; *Augustine, De nupt. et conc.* 1. 23. 25.

⁷⁵ John 6. 6. The heretics inimical to the Old Testament are the Manichaeans. Cf. above, n. 162.

⁷⁶ Here Augustine indicates in a very few words, but quite unmistakably, that he was acquainted with ordeals (*ordalia*) by fire. He uses the term *igne examinari*. In a work translated by Rufinus (*Hist. monach.* 9) we read that the Egyptian monk Copres, engaged in a doctrinal dispute with a Manichaean, proved his orthodoxy by coming through such an ordeal successfully, while his opponent,

who had to be pushed into the fire, burned to death. Gregory
of Tours reports another instance (*In glor. conf.* 14) in which a
Catholic disputant remained unscathed as he retrieved a ring which
had been thrown into the fire. The heretic refused to take the same
risk. Regarding this subject, cf. A. Franz, *Die kirchlichen Bene-
diktionen im Mittelalter* (Freiburg i. Br. 1909) 2. 347-55; A. Michel,
" Ordalies," *Dict. de théol. cath.* 11. 1 (1931) 1139-52.

[77] Eccli. 27. 6.

[78] Gen. 39. 7 ff.

[79] Dan. 13. 19 ff.

[80] Job 1. 11 f. Here we are reminded again that Augustine wrote
the present treatise in the midst of his controversies with the Manichaeans. Cf. above, n. 162.

[81] Isa. 66. 1.

[82] Matt. 5. 34 f.

[83] Rom. 2. 14-16.

[84] *Diabolus*, διάβολος, that is, ' detractor,' ' calumniator,' ' accuser,'
' adversary,' which latter is probably also the basic meaning of the
Hebrew word *Satan*. Cf. W. Foerster, " διάβολος," *Theol. Wörterb. z.
Neuen Test.* 2 (1935) 70-80.

[85] Luke 12. 20.

[86] *Ibid.* 22. 31 f.

[87] 1 Cor. 10. 13. Here the Maurist text and its reproductions in
Migne and Bassi have the subjunctive present *non sinat* (' would not
let ') for the future *non patietur* (' will not suffer ') of the Vulgate.
One might be inclined to take this as a typographical error for *non
sinet* (' will not let '). However, checking parallel uses of this verse
in the *Enarrationes*, we find both the present subjunctive and the
future used in these instances with the present indicative added for
complete measure (61. 20: *non permittit* = ' does not permit ')!

[88] Rom. 8. 24.

[89] ' Ab ipso *humilitatis* Domini adventu agi coepit.' St. Augustine
speaks of the mystery of the Incarnation as *humilitas* (Christ's—God's
—coming in the lowliness of man). Cf. Acts 8. 33 and Phil. 2. 8; also
the remarks of J. P. Christopher, ACW 2 (1946) 130 n. 206.

[90] Cf. John 6. 45 and Isa. 54. 13; cf. above, 2. 6. 20.

[91] Ps. 30. 21.

[92] The mystical significance attached by both pagan and Christian
antiquity to certain numbers is well-known. Cf. J. Sauer, " Zahlensymbolik," *Lex. f. Theol. u. Kirche* 10 (1938) 1025-30; H. Lesêtre,
" Nombre," *Dict. de la Bible* 4 (1908) 1677-97; F. Cabrol, " Nom-

bres," *Dict. d'archéol. chrét. et de lit.* 12. 2 (1936) 1465-9; also the remarks by M. J. Suelzer, ACW 4 (1947) 193 n. 70. For the sacredness of the number " 7 " (*septenarius numerus*) the Fathers found especially numerous indications in the Bible (cf. the passages listed by Sauer, 1027). The passages in which Augustine treats of the *septenarius numerus* are correspondingly frequent; cf. *Quaest. Ev.* 2. 6; *Quaest. in Heptateuch.* 2. 107: *De civ. Dei* 11. 31; *Enarr. in Ps.* 147. 4; etc. See A. Knappitsch, *St. Augustins Zahlensymbolik* (Progr. Graz 1905); A. Schmitt, " Mathematik und Zahlenmystik," in M. Grabmann-J. Mausbach, *Aurelius Augustinus, Festschrift der Görresgesellschaft zum 1500. Jubiläum des heiligen Augustinus* (Cologne 1930) 353-66 (esp. 365). Cf. above, 181 n. 23a; 192 n. 155a.

⁹³ In the following interweaving of the sevenfold Gifts of the Holy Spirit, of seven Beatitudes (the eighth has been termed a reversion to the first: 1. 3. 12), and the seven petitions of the Lord's Prayer, Augustine adheres to his complete inversion (above, 1. 4. 11) of the order in which the *septiformis operatio Spiritus Sancti* is given in Isaias, 11. 2 f. Cf. above, Introduction 7; also 180 n. 17. See R. C. Trench, *Exposition of the Sermon on the Mount Drawn from the Writings of St. Augustine* (3rd ed., London 1869) 174 f.

⁹⁴ Ps. 18. 10.
⁹⁵ Matt. 25. 34.
⁹⁶ Ps. 33. 2.
⁹⁷ Rom. 7. 23 f.
⁹⁸ *Ibid.* 8. 15; Gal. 4. 6.
⁹⁹ Rom. 8. 29.
¹⁰⁰ Matt. 7. 15 f.
¹⁰¹ Eph. 5. 29.
¹⁰² Cf. 1 Cor. 11. 3.
¹⁰³ Isa. 1. 16—according to the Septuagint.
¹⁰⁴ 2 Cor. 3. 18.
¹⁰⁵ Cf. Ps. 118. 36.
¹⁰⁶ 1 Tim. 1. 5.
¹⁰⁷ Among the several variations which these verses show as compared with the Vulgate is the rare word *comestura* = ' wear,' ' corrosion ' (= ' rust '), ' erosion.' Though in a work published some years earlier, the *De vera religione* (4), he already uses the word *aerugo* (= ' rust ') of the Vulgate, here he reverted to the word used in the Old-Latin manuscripts and by St. Cyprian (*De op. et eleem.* 7). Cf. C. H. Milne, *op. cit.* 16.
¹⁰⁸ Ps. 113. 16.

[109] Matt. 24. 35.

[110] Rom. 13. 10.

[111] Col. 3. 5. The Latin term *mortificare*, lit., 'to cause to die' (θανατοῦν—the Germans say 'sich abtöten'), is first found in the Latin versions of the Bible, where it is used often. The word, along with numerous other causative verbs in *-ficare*, is typical of the early Christian vocabulary (Tertullian, Optatus, Ambrose, etc.); cf. C. Mohrmann, *op. cit.* 193, 255 f.; the same, "Quelques observations linguistiques à propos de la nouvelle version latine du psautier," *Vig. Christ.* 1 (1947) 168-70.

[112] Eph. 5. 13.

[113] St. Augustine made himself rather proficient in Greek, but he knew no Hebrew. Still, a native of North Africa, he knew enough Punic to carry on a conversation in the language. Punic was a sister language of Syriac and Hebrew, and thus he frequently attempted to explain difficult Hebrew terms and not without some success. In his seven books, *Locutiones in Heptateuchum*, he undertook to throw light upon obscure expressions in the Pentateuch and the books of Josue and Judges on the basis of Greek and Hebrew idioms. His efforts were not without some fruit. Concerning this interesting sidelight on Augustine's linguistic efforts and accomplishments, cf. H. J. Vogels, "Die Heilige Schrift bei Augustinus," in Grabmann-Mausbach, *Aurelius Augustinus*, 414 f.

[114] *Magistratus huius saeculi* (Vulgate: *princeps huius mundi*): John 12. 31; 14. 30; 16. 11.

[115] Regarding this statement, *nullius enim fere conscientia Deum odisse potest*, the author states in the *Retractationes* (1. 19. 8): 'I realize that it should not have been said. For there are many of whom Scripture says: *The pride of them that hate Thee . . .*' (Ps. 73. 23).

[116] Eccli. 5. 5 f.

[117] Rom. 2. 4. Augustine writes *patientia* for *benignitas* and *invitat* for *adducit* of the Vulgate.

[118] Cf. Rom. 11. 17-24.

[119] Wisd. 1. 1.

[120] In Matt. 6. 25, quoted in §49, the Greek has ψυχή, the Latin, *anima*—both of which mean 'soul'; but both also mean 'life' ('breath of life'), and hence the difficulty to which Augustine refers could arise.

[121] John 12. 25.

[122] Matt. 16. 26.

[123] Cf. Luke 18. 2 ff.

[124] Cf. 1 Cor. 9. 14.

[125] Cf. Acts 20. 34.

[126] 2 Cor. 11. 12.

[127] 1 Cor. 9. 13-15.

[128] *Ibid.* 9. 15.

[129] *Ibid.* 9. 16.

[130] *Ibid.*

[131] *Ibid.*

[132] *Ibid.* 9. 17.

[133] Cf. *ibid.* 4. 1 f.

[134] Matt. 6. 34: *Nolite cogitare de crastino*; the Vulgate: *Nolite ergo soliciti esse in crastinum.*

[135] St. Augustine stated later (*Retract.* 1. 19. 9) that when he wrote this he had overlooked the fact that already our first parents in Paradise had been given food for the body 'before they had merited this penalty of death by sinning. In a body that was not yet spiritual but a living organism, they were, it is true, immortal; yet in such a way that in this their immortality they used food for the body.'

[136] Cf. Matt. 4. 11.

[137] Cf. John 12. 6.

[138] 1 Cor. 16. 1-8.

[139] Acts 11. 27-30. The additions contained in this passage, as compared with the Vulgate, stem from a Greek tradition exemplified in the manuscript kept in Cambridge, the so-called Codex Bezae.

[140] Cf. *ibid.* 28. 10. The reference is to the generosity of the non-Christian natives of the island of Malta. St. Paul had come among them as a result of the foundering of the ship that was bringing him a prisoner to Rome late in the year 60. During his stay there he endeared himself to the islanders by healing many of their sick. When early in 61 the journey was to be resumed and the vessel was about to set sail for Syracuse, they showed their fondness for him and their gratitude by bringing on board gifts and provisions for the voyage.

[141] Eph. 4. 28.

[142] Cf. Acts 20. 33 f.; 1 Cor. 4. 12; 1 Thess. 2. 9; 2 Thess. 3. 8.

[143] That is, tentmakers: cf. Acts 18. 2 f.

[144] Rom. 5. 3-5.

[145] Cf. 2 Cor. 11. 23-27.

[146] As St. Ambrose says (*De excessu fratris sui Satyri* 2. 41), Christ is our physician, and trials and tribulations are the administrations of

His remedy—grace. For the idea of Christ as physician, *medicus*, cf. above, 190 f. n. 144.

147 Matt. 7. 16.

148 I Cor. 5. 12.

149 Rom. 14. 3 f.

150 I Cor. 4. 5.

151 I Tim. 5. 24.

152 *Ibid.* 5. 25.

153 St. Augustine speaks like a true African who venerated his martyrs with remarkable affection and fervor. The present passage brings to mind the celebrated dictum by the African Tertullian (*Apol.* 50), *vincimus cum occidimur*: 'we are victorious as we are slain.' Cf. M. C. D'Arcy, " St. Augustine and His Age," *op. cit.* 54 f.

154 Matt. 26. 52.

155 Christ had foretold to Peter the manner in which he was to die (John 21. 20 f.): "' But when thou shalt be old, thou shalt stretch forth thy hands, and another shall gird thee and lead thee whither thou wouldst not.' And this He said, signifying by what death he should glorify God." Among the early Christian writers Tertullian is the first to refer to Peter's crucifixion: cf. *Scorp.* 15; *De praescr. haer.* 36. Apparently the first witness for the tradition that Peter was crucified with his head downward is Origen, who is quoted by Eusebius, *Hist. eccl.* 3. 1. 2.

156 Cf. Luke 23. 33-43.

157 I Cor. 9. 20-22.

158 *Ibid.* 9. 19.

159 Gal. 5. 13.

160 Cant. 4. 1.

161 Eph. 5. 27. This verse is a favorite with the Fathers in representing the Church as the mystical bride of Christ. Regarding his use of it here, Augustine commented in his *Retractationes* (1. 19. 9) that he had not meant to imply that the Church is in this perfect state now and in all respects. The glory spoken of is attributed to her by way of anticipation: she will be *gloriosa Ecclesia* when Christ will appear in His glory and she with Him. In his treatise, *In Ioan. Ev. tract.* 56. 5, Augustine explains that the Church is already in this condition of a perfect bride—*not having spot or wrinkle*—in those who die immediately after receiving the bath of baptism and those who by God's mercy have quit this life stainless.

162 John 16. 12.

163 I Cor. 3. 1 f.

[164] Matt. 22. 30.
[165] *Ibid.* 22. 21.
[166] *Ibid.* 21. 27.
[167] Cf. John 1. 19-27.
[168] On the dual principle of *actio* and *cognitio* (*contemplatio*) as effecting man's *beatitudo*, cf. also *De agone Christ.* 13. 14; *De civ. Dei* 19. 13. 1 (*pax animae rationalis ordinata cognitionis actionisque consensio*). On the subordination of the one to the other, on *actio* as a preparation for *contemplatio*, see also *De cons. Ev.* 1. 5. 8; *C. Faust. Manich.* 22. 52. Cf. É. Gilson, *Introduction a l'étude de Saint Augustin* (2nd ed., Paris 1943) 153 f.
[169] Regarding this section, St. Augustine later expressed this criticism (*Retract.* 1. 19. 9): "I thought that an elaborate treatment was in place as to how these three should be distinguished; but it is far better to refer them all to the great urgency that should characterize prayer. This (the Lord) showed, too, in the passage in which He embraced all these in one and the same word, saying: *How much more will your Father who is in heaven give good things to them that ask Him* (Matt. 7. 11)? for He did not say—'to them that ask and to them that seek and to them that knock.'"
[170] A conflation of Ps. 23. 1 and 145. 6.
[171] Cyprian has the addition: *De Dom. or.* 28; the Vulgate does not.
[172] Matt. 22. 40.
[173] *Ibid.* 22. 39.
[174] Cf. *ibid.* 22. 40.
[175] Gen. 2. 9.
[176] Matt. 11. 28-30.
[177] To detract from their numerical weakness it was common for heretics to parade themselves as the upper class, the élite, among the Christians. The profounder significance and truths of Christianity, they claimed, were reserved to a select few, and with these they identified themselves—before the masses whom they proselytized. Concerning a certain heretic, probably a Marcionite, Augustine writes (*C. advers. Legis et Prophetarum* 2. 12. 42) that the man in his book 'speaks in high terms of the small following of his heresy—for naturally wisdom is the privilege of the few! This is a common characteristic of the particular vanity of all heretics in their enmity towards the Catholic Church which by her abundant fertility is diffused through all lands. One and all they make a boast of their small numbers and seek out the masses to seduce them.'
[178] St. Augustine refers particularly to Manichaeism and its dual-

istic teaching of a divine world of light and an evil world of darkness. The latter is independent of the former and both are locked in a constant struggle for supremacy. St. Augustine had already written several works (e. g., *De moribus Ecclesiae Catholicae et de moribus Manichaeorum, De Genesi contra Manichaeos, De vera religione*) against the Manichaeans, whom he had once followed; and he lived up to his determination, here expressed, to write further treatises against the sect, if that appeared necessary: note especially his *Contra Faustum Manichaeum*, a very long work written probably in the year 400.

[179] Matt. 12. 33.

[180] *Ibid.* 12. 34.   The Vulgate has 'generation of vipers' for 'hypocrites.'

[181] *Ibid.* 23. 3.

[182] *Ibid.* 23. 2.

[183] Jer. 12. 13.   The Vulgate has the verbs in the third person; the Septuagint, an Old Latin version of which is followed by Augustine, uses the second person.

[184] Matt. 6. 1.

[185] Gal. 5. 19-21.

[186] *Ibid.* 5. 22 f.   Compared with the Vulgate reading, these lists of virtues and vices contain several omissions and transpositions.

[187] The Latin words contrasted are *gaudere* and *gestire*, the latter expressing joy that is unbecomingly demonstrative—extravagant, riotous joy.

[188] Isa. 48. 22 (cf. also 57. 21), according to the Septuagint.

[189] Col. 2. 3.

[190] 1 Cor. 12. 3.

[191] *Ibid.* 13. 6.

[192] Luke 10. 20.

[193] 1 Cor. 6. 9.

[194] Cf. Exod. 7 and 8.

[195] Matt. 24. 23-25.

[196] 2 Tim. 2. 24 f.

[197] It will be recalled that this conclusion also served as the starting-point of the present treatise.

[198] Cf. 1 Cor. 10. 4.

[199] Ps. 11. 6. f.

[200] Isa. 11. 2. Cf. above, 1. 4. 11; also the Introduction 7; again 180 n. 17; 183 n. 57.

INDEX

INDEX

143; after this life, 17; eternal, 39; gradations of, 31 f.
purity, of the heart, 101; of the mind, 125

Quasten, J., 201

raca, ῥακά, ῥάκος, 31, 34, 35, 37, 182
race, human, 186
Rahner, K., 197
rational beings, 136
Raulx, M., 10
reason, reasoning, 16, 120 f., 184
rebirth, 21
reconciliation, 36
Regulator, God, 121
religion, 107
remarriage, 186, 188
rest, everlasting, 146
resurrection, of the body, 111; of the Lord, 21
retaliation, 69 f. See revenge
Reuter, A., 186
revelation, 123
revenge, 117, 190. See retaliation
reward, 96; outward, 128; in heaven, 22
Rhetor ad Herennium, 4. 32. 43: 202
rhetoric, 197
rich, the, obligations of toward the poor, 106
riches, 134. See mammon
right, symbolical, 191
right living, 108. See justice, righteousness
righteousness, 15; of the Pharisees, 81. See justice, right living

robbers, crucified with Christ, 150
rock, Christ, 173
Roland-Gosselin, M. D., 178
Romans, Rome, 197, 206
[Rufinus], *Hist. monach.* 9: 202
rule, of Christian conduct, 78
Runestam, A., 177
Rush, A. C., 198

Sabbath, 21
Sacrament, the, of the Body of the Lord, 113, 115, 124. See Communion
sackcloth, 128
Sadducees, 157
saints, 88, 106; Christians, 187; are God's temple, 107; and sinners, 107
salvation, 91, 157
sanatio, by Christ, 190
sanctimoniousness, 129
sanctitas, sanctificatus, Christianity, Christian, 188
Sanhedrin, 194
sapientia, 7
Sara, 189
Satan, 78, 184, 203; tempter of Job, 120-22. See devil
Sauer, J., 198, 203, 204
scandal, 46 f.
Schaff, D. S., 10
schismatics, 22
Schmitt, A., 204
scholars, 119
Scholastic theologians, 10
Schrijnen, J., 199
Schweitzer, A., 177
scientia, 7
Scribes, 30, 31, 182
Scripture, Sacred, 13, 17, 19, 39,